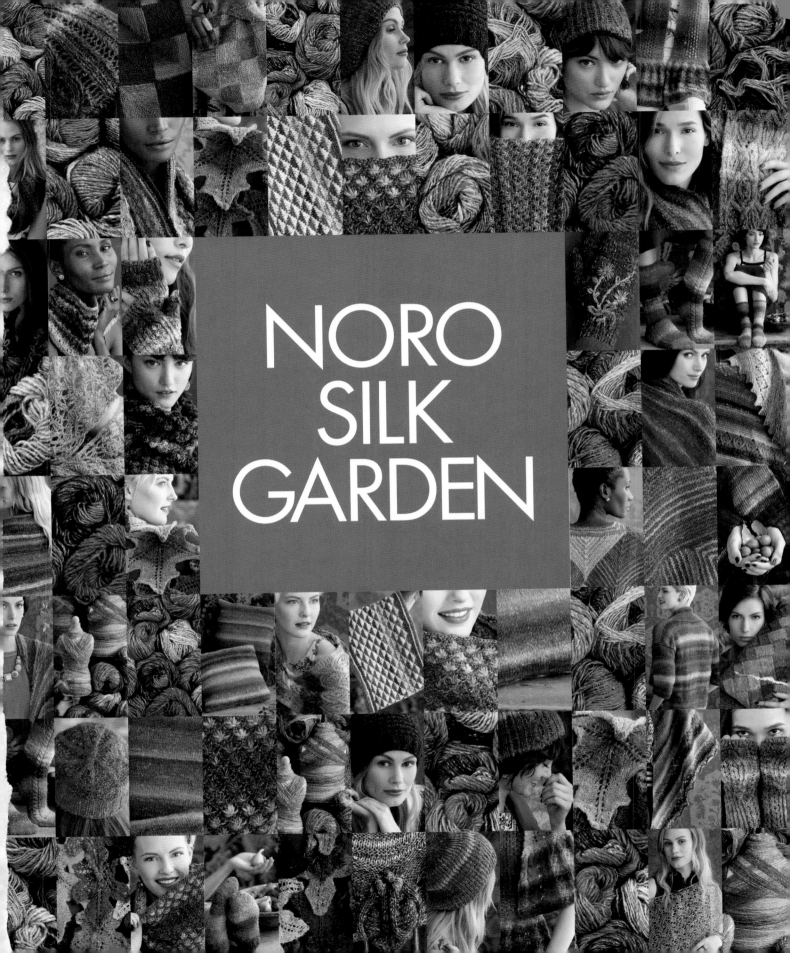

NORO
SILK
GARDEN

NORO
SILK
GARDEN

THE 20TH ANNIVERSARY
COLLECTION

Editor
PAMELA WYNNE
BUTLER

Yarn Editor
MATTHEW SCHRANK

Editorial Assistant
JACOB SEIFERT

Supervising Patterns
Editor
CARLA SCOTT

Instructions Editor
MARI LYNN PATRICK

Instructions Assistant
CEVRI CIVELEK

Technical Illustrations
LORETTA DACHMAN

Photography
JACK DEUTSCH

Set Design Assistant
WILLIAM MARPLE

Stylist
JOANNA RADOW

Assistant Stylist
EMILY WHITTED

Hair and Makeup
ELENA LYAKIR
INGEBORG

Vice President/
Editorial Director
TRISHA MALCOLM

Publisher
CAROLINE KILMER

Creative Director
JOE VIOR

Production Manager
DAVID JOINNIDES

President
ART JOINNIDES

Chairman
JAY STEIN

Library of Congress Cataloging-in-Publication Data
Title: Noro Silk Garden : the 25th anniversary collection/
the editors of Sixth&Spring Books.
Description: First edition. New York : Sixth&Spring
Books, [2016] Includes index.
Identifiers: LCCN 2015035891 ISBN 9781942021902
(hardcover)
Subjects: LCSH: Knitting–Patterns.
Yarn–Materials. Silk. Mohair. Worsted. Eisaku Noro, Ltd.
Classification: LCC TT825 .N66 2016 DDC 746.43/2–dc23
LC record available at http://lccn.loc.gov/2015035891

Manufactured in China

1 3 5 7 9 10 8 6 4 2

First Edition

CONTENTS

The Story of Silk Garden

The origin of Silk Garden yarn is tied to the history of silk and fabric in Japan. As I created it, I remembered my own experiences with fiber and fabric over many decades.

My history with silk began 70 years ago, when I was a child. At farms, mulberries were grown to feed and raise silkworms as a side business. The silkworms were nurtured in well-ventilated places in summer. In fall, when it grew colder, the entire house was kept warm for them. Silkworms were taken care of by the entire family, including grandparents and children. Silk was woven into everyday life.

My history with fabric goes back 50 years, to my adolescence. Shaggy mohair fabric and coats were very popular then. When the sheen and luster of mohair is blended with silk, then dyed, the fabric blossoms into a mélange of shaded color.

Silk Garden is a blend of silk and mohair with lambswool. The unique depth of its colors comes from the combination of these raw materials.

Imagine a garden of silk.

Silk Garden is the name I gave to this yarn as I remembered the past, imagining a yarn that bloomed out of a garden of silk and silk-mohair fabric.

Eisaku Noro

The Projects

Mitered Squares Blanket

Mitered Squares Blanket

Designed by Bonnie Franz

Garter-stitch squares, knit using the mitered technique, alternate one solid block with one multicolored block. The squares are continuously joined to make up this gorgeous heirloom blanket design.

Skill Level
■■□□

Size
Instructions are written for one size.

Knitted Measurements
Approx 45"/114cm square
Each square measures 5½"/14cm square

Materials
- 8 1¾oz/50g balls (each approx 110yd/100m) of Noro *Silk Garden* (silk/mohair/wool) in #08 Royal (A)
- 8 1¾oz/50g balls (each approx 110yd/100m) of Noro *Silk Garden Solo* (silk/mohair/wool) in #03 Royal (B)
- One size 8 (5mm) circular needle, 32"/80cm long, OR SIZE TO OBTAIN GAUGE
- Stitch markers

Gauge
16 sts and 32 rows to 4"/10cm over garter st using size 8 (5mm) needles. TAKE TIME TO CHECK GAUGE.

Note
After working the first square, each consecutive square in the first line of squares is worked by picking up sts along the side edge of the previous square, then casting on the corner and straight edge sts to cont working the new square. The next line of squares (after the first square) will then be joined into the first worked square and the previous line of squares. Use the diagram to see the square and line layout and color placements.

Blanket
Line 1
Square 1

With A, cast on 20 sts, pm on needle, cast on 3 sts, pm on needle, cast on 20 sts–43 sts.
Row 1 (WS) Knit, slipping the markers.
Row 2 (RS) K to marker, sl marker, SK2P, sl marker, k to end.
Row 3 (WS) K to 1 st before marker, place new marker, k3 (removing previous markers), place new marker, k to end.
Rep rows 2 and 3 until only 1 st rem. Cut yarn, leaving a long end for weaving in later.

Square 2

With B and with 1 st on needle, from the RS, pick up and k 19 more sts along the side edge of square 1, pm, cast on 3 sts, pm, cast on 20 sts–43 sts.
Row 1 (WS) Knit, slipping the markers.
Rep rows 2 and 3 of Square 1 until only 1 st rem. Cut yarn, leaving a long end for weaving in later.

Squares 3–8

Work as for Square 2, foll diagram for colors. On Square 8, fasten off the last st. This completes Line 1.

Line 2
Square 9

With B, cast on 20 sts, pm, cast on 3 sts, pm, then from the RS, pick up and k 20 sts along the bottom edge of Square 1.
Knit 1 row, then rep rows 2 and 3 of Square 1 until only 1 st rem. Cut yarn, leaving a long end for weaving in later.

Square 10

With A and with 1 st on needle, from the RS, pick up and k 19 more sts along the inside edge of Square 9, pm, pick up and k 3 sts along the inside edge of corner, pm, pick up and k 20 sts along the bottom edge of Square 2. Knit 1 row, then rep rows 2 and 3 of Square 1 until only 1 st rem.

Squares 11–40

Alternating A and B as shown on the diagram, and using the 2-sided joining (as on Square 10) on all inside squares, and one-sided joining (as on Square 9) on Squares 17, 25 and 33, work these 4 lines foll the diagram. Lines 2–5 are complete.

Line 6

Square 41

With A, cast on 20 sts, pm, cast on 3 sts, pm, rotate the needle with cast-on sts to the WS and, with the RS of blanket facing, pick up and k 20 sts along top edge of Square 8. Knit 1 row, then rep rows 2 and 3 of Square 1 until only 1 st rem. Cut yarn, leaving a long end for weaving in later.

Square 42

With B and with 1 st on needle, from the RS, pick up and k 19 more sts along the inside edge of Square 41, pm, pick up and k 3 sts along the inside edge of corner, pm, pick up and k 20 sts along the top edge of Square 7. Knit 1 row, then rep rows 2 and 3 of Square 1 until only 1 st rem.

Squares 43–64

Alternating A and B as shown on the diagram, and using the 2-sided joining (as on square 42) on all inside squares, and one-sided joining (as on square 41) on Squares 49 and 57, work these 3 lines foll the diagram. Lines 6–8 are complete.

Finishing

Weave in ends, then block to finished measurements.

Side Trim

With A, from the RS, pick up and k 22 sts along each square for 176 total sts. Knit 3 rows. Bind off knitwise. Rep on other side.

Lower and Top Trim

With B, work the same as for side trim picking up 2 extra sts along edge of side trim to close up corners—180 total sts. Knit 3 rows. Bind off knitwise. Weave in ends and lightly block entire piece again. ✤

DIAGRAM

↘ Direction of work | First pick-up edge, square 2

Stained Glass Windows Hat

Stained Glass Windows Hat

Designed by Theresa Schabes

Reflect your style with two coordinating colorways—one solid and one multi-colored—in this slouchy winter hat.

Skill Level
■■□□

Size
Instructions are written for one size.

Knitted Measurements
Circumference 19"/48cm
Height 9"/23cm

Materials
- 1 1¾oz/50g ball (each approx 110yd/100m) of Noro *Silk Garden Solo* (silk/mohair/wool) in #07 Red (A) (4)
- 1 1¾oz/50g ball (each approx 110yd/100m) of Noro *Silk Garden* (silk/mohair/wool) in #394 Gold/Green/Brown/Black/Blue (B) (4)
- One each sizes 6 and 8 (4 and 5mm) circular needles, 16"/40cm long, OR SIZE TO OBTAIN GAUGE
- One set (5) size 8 (5mm) double-pointed needles (dpn)
- Stitch marker
- Waste yarn

Gauge
17 sts and 29 rnds to 4"/10cm over stained glass pat using larger circular needle. TAKE TIME TO CHECK GAUGE.

Tubular Cast-on
1) With contrasting waste yarn, cast on half the required stitches, plus one extra, using a backwards loop cast-on. (For example, if the final cast-on is 80, cast on 40+1 = 41 sts.) Cut the yarn.
2) Join the main yarn and work as follows: k1, *bring yarn to front, k1 (creating a yo around the needle); rep from * to last st, do *not* bring yarn to front, end k1.
3) On next row, k1, *k1, bring yarn to front, sl next stitch purlwise, bring yarn to back; rep from * to last st, k1.
4) On next row, bring yarn to front, *sl 1, bring yarn to back, k1, bring yarn to front; rep from * to last stitch, k1.
Cont in designated pattern. After a few rows in pattern, carefully cut and remove the waste yarn.

Stained Glass Pattern Stitch
(multiple of 9 sts)
Rnds 1 and 2 With A, knit.
Rnd 3 With B, *sl 2 wyib, k1, [sl 1 wyif, k1] 3 times; rep from * around.
Rnd 4 With B, *sl 2 wyib, k7; rep from * around.
Rnd 5 With A, *k2, sl 1 wyif, [k1, sl 1 wyif] 3 times; rep from * around.
Rnd 6 With A, knit.
Rnd 7 Rep rnd 3.
Rnd 8 Rep rnd 4.
Rnd 9 Rep rnd 5.
Rnd 10 Rep rnd 6.
Rnd 11 Rep rnd 3.
Rnd 12 Rep rnd 4.
Rnd 13 Rep rnd 5.
Rnd 14 Rep rnd 6.
Rep rnds 1–14 for stained glass pat st.

Hat
With smaller circular needle and A, cast on for a final amount of 80 sts using the tubular cast-on method. After completing steps 1–4 in rows in the tubular cast-on, join to work in rnds and pm to mark beg of rnd, taking care not to twist sts on needle. Work in k2, p2 rib as foll:
Next rnd *K2, p2; rep from * around.
Rep this rnd for k2, p2 rib until piece measures 2"/5cm from beg, inc 1 st on the last rnd—81 sts. Change to larger circular needle.
Begin Stained Glass Pattern Stitch
Beg with rnd 1, work 3 reps of the 14-rnd pat st.

Crown Shaping
Note Divide sts evenly over 4 dpn when there are too few sts to fit comfortably on the circular needle.
Dec rnd 1 With A, [k7, k2tog] 9 times—72 sts.
Rnd 2 With A, knit.

Dec rnd 3 With B, *sl 2 wyib, [k1, sl 1 wyif] twice, k2tog; rep from * 8 times more—63 sts.

Rnd 4 With B, *sl 2 wyib, k5; rep from * around.

Rnd 5 With A, *k2, sl 1 wyif, [k1, sl 1 wyif] twice; rep from * around.

Dec rnd 6 With A, [k5, k2tog] 9 times—54 sts.

Dec rnd 7 With B, *sl 2 wyib, k1, sl 1 wyif, k2tog; rep from * 8 times more—45 sts.

Rnd 8 With B, *sl 2 wyib, k3; rep from * around.

Rnd 9 With A, *k2, sl 1 wyif, k1, sl 1 wyif; rep from * around.

Dec rnd 10 With A, [k2, k2tog, k1] 9 times—36 sts.

Dec rnd 11 With B, [sl 2 wyib, k2tog] 9 times—27 sts.

Rnd 12 With A, knit.

Dec rnd 13 With A, [k1, ssk] 9 times—18 sts.

Rnd 14 With A, knit.

Last rnd With A, [k2tog] 9 times—9 sts.

Cut yarn, leaving a long end. Pull through sts on needles once, then pull through sts again and draw up tightly to close top.

Finishing

Weave in ends and block hat to knitted measurements. ✤

Starburst Cowl

Starburst Cowl

Designed by Irina Poludnenko

Inspired by the facets of modern jewelry, this statement cowl swaps minerals and gemstones for hand-knit colors and textures.

Skill Level

Size
Instructions are written for one size.

Knitted Measurements
Circumference 27"/68.5cm
Height 10"/25.5cm

Materials
- 1 1¾oz/50g ball (each approx 110yd/100m) of Noro *Silk Garden Solo* (silk/mohair/wool) in #04 Olive Green (A) (4)
- 2 1¾oz/50g balls (each approx 110yd/100m) of Noro *Silk Garden* (silk/mohair/wool) in #341 Reds/Burgundy/Mustard (B) (4)
- One size 8 (5mm) circular needle, 24"/60cm long, OR SIZE TO OBTAIN GAUGE
- Stitch marker

Gauge
20 sts and 22 rnds to 4"/10cm over starburst pat st using size 8 (5mm) needle. TAKE TIME TO CHECK GAUGE.

Starburst Pattern Stitch
(multiple of 6 sts)
Cast on with A and purl 1 rnd.
Rnd 1 With B, *sl 1 wyib, loosely k5; rep from * around.
Rnd 2 With B, *sl 1 wyib, k5tog but do not sl the sts from LH needle, then (yo, k5tog, yo, k5tog) in the same 5 sts; rep from * around.
Rnd 3 With A, knit.
Rnd 4 With A, purl.
Rnd 5 With B, loosely k3, *sl 1 wyib, loosely k5; rep from *, end last rep with loosely k2 instead of k5.
Rnd 6 With B, (k3tog, yo, k3tog) in the same first 3 sts, *sl 1 st wyib, k5tog but do not sl the sts from LH needle, then (yo, k5tog, yo, k5tog) in the same 5 sts; rep from * to the last 2 sts, end last rep with k2tog, but do not sl the sts from LH needle, then k the first st again.
Rnd 7 With A, knit.
Rnd 8 With A, purl.
Rep rnds 1–8 for starburst pat st.

Cowl
With A, cast on 132 sts loosely. Join to work in rnds, taking care not to twist sts, and pm to mark beg of rnd. Purl 1 rnd.
Begin Starburst Pattern Stitch
Work in starburst pat st, rep rnds 1–8 for a total of 7 reps. Bind off loosely knitwise with A.

Finishing
Weave in ends and block piece to knitted measurements. ❖

Asymmetric Lace Shawl

Asymmetric Lace Shawl

Designed by Anniken Allis

Start small and end big with a design that builds on one edge to create this dramatic asymmetrical shawl.

Skill Level

■■■□

Size

Instructions are written for one size.

Knitted Measurements

Length (at top edge) 72"/183cm
Depth (at widest point) 20"/51cm

Materials

- 2 3½oz/100g balls (each approx 328yd/300m) of Noro *Silk Garden Sock* (wool/silk/polyamide/mohair) in #420 Purple/Grey/Green
- One pair size 6 (4mm) needles, OR SIZE TO OBTAIN GAUGE
- One size 6 (4mm) circular needle, 32"/80cm long

Stitch Glossary

Kfbf K1 into front, back, and front of st (inc 2 sts)
RBO (Russian bind-off) K2, sl both sts back to LH needle, k2tog tbl, *k1, sl both sts back to LH needle, k2tog tbl; rep from * until all sts are bound off.

Gauge

16 sts and 30 rows to 4"/10cm over garter st, after blocking, using size 6 (4mm) needles. TAKE TIME TO CHECK GAUGE.

Garter Stitch Pattern

Row 1 (RS) Sl 1 wyif, kfbf, k to end—2 sts inc'd.
Rows 2, 4 and 6 (WS) Sl 1 wyif, k to end.
Row 3 Sl 1 wyif, kfbf, k to end—2 sts inc'd.
Row 5 Sl 1 wyif, kfbf, k to end—2 sts inc'd.
Row 7 Sl 1 wyif, kfbf, k to end—2 sts inc'd.
Row 8 RBO 4, k to end—4 sts dec'd.
Rep these 8 rows for garter st pat rep. 4 sts added to the st count over each 8-row rep.

Shawl

Cast on 2 sts. Knit 1 row on WS.
Row 1 (RS) Sl 1 wyif, kfbf—4 sts.
Rows 2, 4 and 6 (WS) Sl 1 wyif, k to end.
Row 3 Sl 1 wyif, kfbf, k2—6 sts.
Row 5 Sl 1 wyif, kfbf, k to end—8 sts.
Row 7 Sl 1 wyif, kfbf, k to end—10 sts.
Row 8 RBO 4, k to end—6 sts.
Cont in pat as foll:
Work the 8-row rep of garter st pat for a total of 11 times—50 sts.
Work rows 1–16 of chart 1 once—58 sts.
Work the 8-row rep of garter st pat for a total of 6 times—82 sts.
Work rows 1–16 of chart 1 once—90 sts.
Work the 8-row rep of garter st pat for a total of 6 times—114 sts.
Work rows 1–16 of chart 1 once—122 sts.
Work the 8-row rep of garter st pat for a total of 6 times—146 sts.
Work rows 1–16 of chart 1 once—154 sts.
Work the 8-row rep of garter st pat for a total of 2 times—162 sts.
Work rows 1–16 of chart 2 once—174 sts.
Bind off all sts loosely using the Russian bind-off.

Finishing

Weave in ends and block shawl to measurements, pinning points out to create the jagged edges. ❖

CHART 1

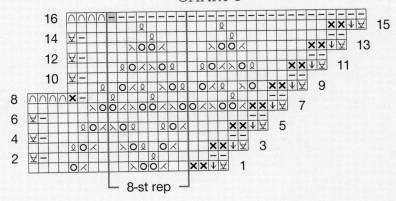

8-st rep

CHART 2

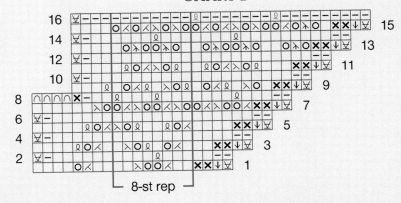

8-st rep

STITCH KEY

- ☐ k on RS, p on WS
- ⊟ p on RS, k on WS
- ⊙ yo
- ⊠ k2tog
- ⊠ ssk
- ⋔ SK2P
- ⊻ slip 1 wyif
- ↓ kfbf
- ℓ k1 tbl on RS, p1 tbl on WS
- ℓ k1 tbl on WS
- ⌒ RBO
- ☒ st made by kfbf
  or left from last RBO
- ⬛ applies to first pat rep only

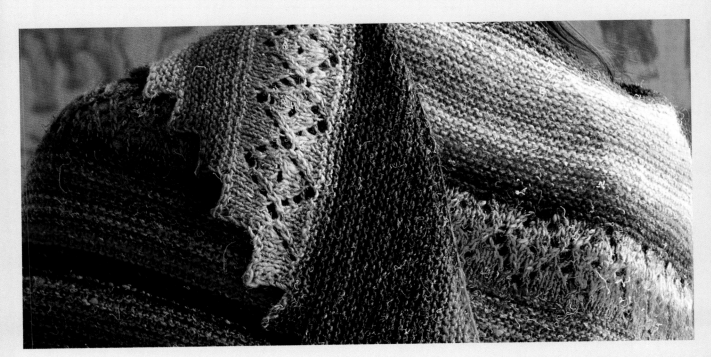

Japanese Knot Bag

Japanese Knot Bag

Designed by Jacqueline van Dillen

This entrelac handbag is worked almost seamlessly in two pieces, making finishing a snap. A sewn-in cotton lining adds durability and helps the bag keep its shape.

Skill Level
■■■■

Size
Instructions are written for one size.

Knitted Measurements
Width 14"/36cm
Depth (short side) 17"/43cm
Depth (long side) 21"/53cm
One entrelac square measures 2½"/6.5cm square

Materials
- 3 1¾oz/50g balls (each approx 110yd/100m) of Noro *Silk Garden* (silk/mohair/wool) each in #341 Reds/Burgundy/Mustard (A) and #279 Browns/Blues/Deep Rose (B) (④)
- One pair of size 6 (4mm) needles, OR SIZE TO OBTAIN GAUGE
- 1yd/1m of cotton lining fabric
- ½yd/.5m of ¼"/6mm flexible flat plastic strip (for top reinforcement)

Gauge
20 sts and 40 rows to 4"/10cm over garter st using size 6 (4mm) needles. TAKE TIME TO CHECK GAUGE.

Notes
1) Bag is worked using the entrelac method, with triangles and squares worked directionally, and adding each segment onto previous segment.
2) For ease in working, use a small length of a contrasting color yarn to mark the right-side of the piece.
3) If desired, when picking up sts from the WS in a different color, pick up and purl the sts to eliminate the purl bump in the opposite color on the RS.
4) Final instructions and diagram can be found on page 138.

Front
With A, cast on 36 sts.
Base Triangles
First Base Triangle
Next row (RS) With A, k2, turn work; k2, turn work.
Next row (RS) K3, turn work; k3, turn work.
Next row (RS) K4, turn work; k4, turn work.
Cont to work these 2 RS and WS rows in garter st, always adding one more st on the RS row, until there are a total of 12 sts on the RH needle, ending with a RS row. Do *not* turn on this last RS row. These 12 sts will be kept on hold on the needle while working the second and third triangles.
Second Base Triangle
Work as for first base triangle.
Third Base Triangle
Work as for first base triangle. First row of base triangles is complete. Cut A.

First Row of Squares
First Square
With B, cast on 12 sts onto empty needle and, beg with a WS row, k12, turn, k12, turn.
Next row (WS) K11, work ssk with the last B st and first A st from the previous triangle, turn, k12, turn.
Rep the last 2 rows until all sts from the square are joined to the sts from the triangle. Do *not* turn on the last WS row.
Second Square
With B, from the WS, pick up and k 12 sts along the other edge of the triangle just worked into.
Next row (RS) K12, turn.
Next row (WS) K11, work ssk with the last B st and first A st from the 2nd triangle, turn.
Rep the last 2 rows until all sts from the square are joined to the sts from the triangle, do *not* turn on the last WS row.

Third Square
With B, working from the WS of the 2nd triangle and into the outer edge, pick up and k 12 sts along this edge.
Next row (RS) K12, turn.
Next row (WS) K11, work ssk with the last B st and first A st from the 3rd triangle, turn.
Rep the last 2 rows until all sts from the square are joined to the sts from the triangle. Do *not* turn on the last WS row.
Fourth Square
With B, working from the WS, pick up and k 12 sts along the other edge of the triangle just worked into.
Next row (RS) K12, turn.
Next row (WS) K12, turn.
Rep last 2 rows until 24 rows are worked in garter st. Do *not* turn. Cut B. First row of squares is complete.

Second Row of Squares
Note The second row of squares begins with a triangle to fill in the edge, and ends with another triangle to fill in the opposite edge. Refer to the diagram.
Beg Side Triangle
Next row (RS) With A, k2, turn.
Next row (WS) K2, turn.
Next row (RS) Kfb, k the last st tog with 1 st from top of the previous row's square, turn, k3, turn.
Next row (RS) Kfb, k1, k the last st tog with 1 st from top of the previous square, turn, k4, turn.
Next row (RS) Kfb, k to the last A st, k the last st tog with 1 st from top of the previous square, turn.
Next row (WS) Knit.
Rep last 2 rows until all sts from the previous square are worked into. Work last RS row as foll: Kfb, k9, k2tog, do *not* turn—12 sts on RH needle.

Second Row Squares
Work 3 squares, joining with k2tog instead of ssk as for previous row of squares and picking up sts along the RS, not WS, of piece.

End Side Triangle
With A, from the RS, pick up and k 12 sts along the side edge of the first square from the first row of the squares.
Next row (WS) K2tog, k10, turn, k11, turn.
Next row (WS) K2tog, k9, turn, k10, turn.
Rep these 2 rows, always dec'ing 1 st as established every WS row, until 2 sts rem, ending with a RS row. Cut A.
Next row (WS) With B, k2tog, do *not* turn. Second row of squares is complete.

Third Row of Squares
With the 1 st rem on needle from previous row and B, from the WS, pick up and k 11 sts along the side edge of the triangle for 12 sts total.

Next row (RS) K12, turn.
Next row (WS) K to the last B st, work ssk with the last B st and first A st from the previous square, turn, k12.
Cont to work in this way, joining as for previous squares until all 12 sts are joined. Do *not* turn on the last WS row. Work 3 more squares as previously established to complete third row of squares.

Foll the diagram, rep the second row of squares, then rep the third row of squares.
Foll the diagram, rep the second row of squares again, working only the beg side triangle and one square.

Top RS Triangle
With A, from the RS, pick up and k 12 sts along the side of the square from previous row of squares. K12, turn.
Next row (RS) K2tog, k9, k2tog the last st with 1 st from previous square, turn, k11, turn.
Next row (RS) K2tog, k8, k the last st on needle tog with 1 st from previous square, turn, k10, turn.
Cont to work in this way until all sts from the previous square have been worked into.

With 1 st rem on needle from top RS triangle and from the RS, pick up and k 11 sts along the side of previous square, k12, turn.
Foll the diagram, work final square and end side triangle to complete row.

Long Handle
Foll the diagram as well as the directional working from the previous rows, (work a third row square followed by a beg and end side triangle) twice.

Top WS Triangle
With B, from the WS, pick up and k 12 sts along the side of the triangle from previous row of side triangles. K12, turn.
Next row (RS) K2tog, k9, ssk the last st with 1 st from previous triangle, turn, k11, turn.
Next row (RS) K2tog, k8, ssk the last st on needle tog with 1 st from previous triangle, turn, k10, turn. Cont to work in this way until all sts from the previous triangle have been worked into.

Short Handle
With A, bind off 12 sts from square from previous row of squares. Foll the diagram as well as the directional working from the previous rows, work one more square, one more set of beg and end side triangles, and one top WS triangle.

Back
Work as for Front, reversing the placement of the long and short handles to match Front. (Instructions continued on page 138.)

Drape Front Cardigan

Drape Front Cardigan

Designed by Theresa Schabes

Form meets function in this simple, open cardigan with a wedge-shaped back and directionally knit fronts.

Skill Level

■ ■ ■ □

Sizes
Instructions are written for size X-Small (Small, Medium, Large, X-Large, XX-Large). Shown in size Small.

Knitted Measurements
Bust (closed) 34 (36, 38, 40½, 42, 45)"/86 (91.5, 96.5, 103, 106.5, 114)cm
Length 24¼ (24¾, 25¼, 25¾, 26¼, 26¾)"/61.5 (63, 64, 65.5, 66.5, 68)cm
Upper arm 13½ (14½, 15, 16½, 17¼, 18)"/34 (37, 38, 42, 44, 46)cm

Materials
- 3 (3, 4, 4, 4, 5) 3½oz/100g balls (each approx 328yd/300m) of Noro *Silk Garden Sock Solo* (wool/silk/polyamide/mohair) in #3 Royal (A) ②
- 2 (2, 2, 3, 3, 3) 3½oz/100g balls (each approx 328yd/300m) of Noro *Silk Garden Sock* (wool/silk/polyamide/mohair) in #354 Purple/Green/Blues (B) ②
- One pair each sizes 4 and 6 (3.5 and 4mm) needles, OR SIZE TO OBTAIN GAUGE

- One set (5) each sizes 4 and 6 (3.5 and 4mm) double-pointed needles (dpn)
- One size 4 (3.5mm) circular needle, 29"/74cm long
- Stitch markers

Gauge
19 sts and 28 rows/rnds to 4"/10cm over St st, using larger needles.
TAKE TIME TO CHECK GAUGE.

Seed Stitch Pattern
(even number of sts)
Row 1 (RS) *K1, p1; rep from * to end.
Row 2 K the purl and p the knit sts.
Rep row 2 for seed st pattern.

Notes
1) This cardigan is constructed beginning at the lower back edge with A and is knit with wedge increase shaping up to the armhole. Stitches are then bound off straight at the underarm, and the back armhole is worked partially in St st and partially in seed st. Then, after shaping the back neck, the 2 shoulder edges are each decreased to a single point with 2 sts on each side. Stitches are then picked up around the armhole opening, formed with the back shoulder edge that wraps around to the front, and sleeves are worked from the top down in rounds to each sleeve cuff edge. Finally, each front edge is worked in B straight across to the center, beginning by picking up sts along the angled back and the shoulder edge. See schematic.
2) One selvage st on each edge of back piece is not calculated into the schematic measurements.
3) Second diagram can be found on page 138.

Back
With smaller needles and A, cast on 30 (34, 34, 38, 38, 42) sts.
Row 1 (RS) K2, *p2, k2; rep from * to end.
Row 2 P2, *k2, p2; rep from * to end.
Rep these 2 rows for k2, p2 rib for 1½"/4cm.
Change to larger needles and, beg with a RS (knit) row, work in St st for 4 rows.
Inc row (RS) K1, kfb, k to the last 3 sts, kfb, k2.
Rep inc row every 4th row 6 (5, 5, 4, 0, 0) times more, then work the inc row (every alternate 2nd and 4th row) for a total of 22 (24, 26, 28, 34, 35) times—88 (94, 98, 104, 108, 114) sts.
Work even until piece measures 17¾"/45cm from beg.

Armhole Shaping

Bind off 8 sts at beg of next 2 rows—72 (78, 82, 88, 92, 98) sts. Work even for 2 (2½, 3, 3½, 4, 4½)"/5 (6.5, 7.5, 9, 10, 11.5) cm. Change to smaller needles and work in seed st pat until armhole measures 5 (5½, 6, 6½, 7, 7½)"/12.5 (14, 15, 16.5, 18, 19) cm. **Note** Piece will cont in seed st to end.

Back Neck Shaping

Next row (RS) Work 29 (31, 33, 35, 37, 39) sts in seed st, join a 2nd ball of A and bind off center 14 (16, 16, 18, 18, 20) sts, work in seed st to end. Working both sides at once, bind off 4 sts from each neck edge twice, 2 sts once and 1 st once—18 (20, 22, 24, 26, 28) sts rem each side.
Cont to shape each side piece, dec'ing 1 st from each (inside) neck edge every 4th row 10 (8, 6, 4, 2, 0) times then every 3rd row 6 (10, 14, 18, 22, 26) times. Bind off rem 2 sts each side for top of armhole.

Sleeves

With larger dpn, locate the center of the 8-st armhole bind-off. With RS facing and A, pick up and k 64 (68, 72, 78, 82, 86) sts around armhole, ending by picking up rem sts from 8-st armhole bind-off. Divide sts evenly onto 4 dpn, join, and pm to mark beg of rnd. Work 8 rnds in St st (k every rnd).
Dec rnd K2tog, k to last 2 sts, ssk.
Rep dec rnd every 10th rnd 11 (11, 11, 0, 0, 0) times more then every 8th rnd 0 (0, 0, 14, 14, 14) times—40 (44, 48, 48, 52, 56) sts. Work even until sleeve measures 18½"/47cm from beg. Change to smaller dpn and work in k2, p2 rib for 1½"/4cm. Bind off in rib. Work 2nd sleeve in same way.

Left Front

Place marker along the front neck edge at 6½ (7, 7½, 8, 8½, 9)"/16.5 (18, 19, 20.5, 21.5, 23) cm from the bottom of armhole (see purple line on schematic to right and page 138). Beg at this marker with larger needles and B, pick up and k 104 (106, 109, 112, 114, 117) sts (approx 2 sts for every 3 rows) moving towards the back piece's cast-on edge.
Row 1 (WS) K8 (for lower trim), p to end.
Row 2 (RS) Knit.
Rep these 2 rows until piece measures 14½ (15, 15½, 16, 16½, 17)"/37 (38, 39.5, 40.5, 42, 43) cm from the pick-up edge. Change to smaller needles and, with A, work as foll:
Row 1 (RS) Knit.
Row 2 (WS) Sl 1, p2 (k2, p2, p2, k2, p2), then work in k2, p2 rib to the last 5 (5, 6, 5, 5, 6) sts, end k2, p3 (p3, p4, p3, p3, p4). Cont in k2, p2 rib as established for 1"/2.5 cm. Bind off in rib.

Right Front

Work as for left front in reverse. Place marker, begin picking up sts at lower edge of back and ending at marker.
Row 1 (WS) P to last 8 sts, k8 (for lower trim).
Row 2 (RS) Knit.
Complete as for left front.

Finishing

With RS facing, circular needle and A, pick up approx 2 sts for every 3 rows and k 172 (176, 180, 188, 192, 196) sts from the lower edge of the right front, around the neck edge and to the lower edge of the left front.
Row 1 (WS) Sl 1, *p2, k2; rep from * to last 3 sts, p3.
Row 2 (RS) Sl 1, *k2, p2; rep from * to last 3 sts, end k3.
Rep these 2 rows for k2, p2 rib for 1"/2.5 cm. Bind off in rib. Weave in ends and block finished cardigan to measurements. ✤

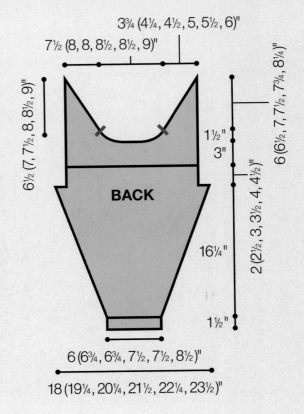

3¾ (4¼, 4½, 5, 5½, 6)"

7½ (8, 8, 8½, 8½, 9)"

6½ (7, 7½, 8, 8½, 9)"

6 (6½, 7, 7½, 7¾, 8¼)"

1½"

3"

2 (2½, 3, 3½, 4, 4½)"

BACK

16¼"

1½"

6 (6¾, 6¾, 7½, 7½, 8½)"

18 (19¼, 20¼, 21½, 22¼, 23½)"

Cable-Detailed Socks

Cable-Detailed Socks

Designed by Zabeth Loisel-Weiner

Simple cables twine up the sides of these colorful socks, which will fit a wide range of feet—the pattern is written for three sizes, and is customizable to any foot length.

Skill Level

■ ■ ■ □

Sizes

Instructions are written for woman's size Small (Medium, Large) width. Shown in size Medium.
Note For sock length, adjust when indicated in the instructions.

Knitted Measurements

Foot circumference 6½ (7½, 8½)"/16.5 (19, 21.5) cm
Foot length Custom

Materials

■ 1 3½oz/100g ball (each approx 328yd/300m) of Noro *Silk Garden Sock* (wool/silk/polyamide/mohair) in #420 Purple/Grey/Green
■ One set (4) size 3 (3.25mm) double pointed needles (dpn),
OR SIZE TO OBTAIN GAUGE
■ Waste yarn
■ Stitch markers
■ Cable needle (cn)
■ Tapestry needle

Provisional Cast-on

Using waste yarn and crochet hook, chain the number of sts to cast on, plus a few extra. Cut a tail and pull the tail through the last chain. With knitting needle and working yarn, pick up and knit the stated number of sts through the "purl bumps" on the back of the chain. To remove waste yarn chain, when instructed, pull out the tail from the last crochet stitch. Gently and slowly pull on the tail to unravel the crochet stitches, carefully placing each released knit stitch on the knitting needle.

Kitchener Stitch

1) Divide stitches evenly between two knitting needles. Hold needles parallel. Insert tapestry needle purlwise through first stitch on front needle. Pull yarn through, leaving that stitch on knitting needle.
2) Insert tapestry needle knitwise through first stitch on back needle. Pull yarn through, leaving stitch on knitting needle.
3) Insert tapestry needle knitwise through first stitch on front needle, slip stitch off needle. Insert tapestry needle purlwise through next stitch on front needle. Pull yarn through, leaving stitch on needle.
4) Insert tapestry needle purlwise through first stich on back needle, slipping stitch off needle. Insert tapestry needle knitwise through next stitch on back needle. Pull yarn through, leaving stitch on needle. Repeat steps 3 and 4 until all stitches on front and back needles have been grafted. Fasten off and weave in end.

Stitch Glossary

M1R (make 1 right) Insert LH needle from back to front under the horizontal bar between the last st worked and the next st on LH needle, k1 through the front loop to M1R.
M1L (make 1 left) Insert LH needle from front to back under the horizontal bar between the last st worked and the next st on LH needle, k1 through back loop to M1L.

Short Row Wrap & Turn (w & t)

On RS row (on WS row)
1) Wyib (wyif), sl next st purlwise.
2) Move yarn between the needles to the front (back).
3) Sl the same st back to LH needle, turn work. One st is wrapped.
4) When working the wrapped st, insert RH needle under the wrap and work it tog with the corresponding st on needle.

Gauge

22 sts and 40 rnds to 4"/10cm over St st using size 3 (3.25mm) dpn.
TAKE TIME TO CHECK GAUGE.

Right Cable Pattern

(worked in rnds over a panel of 6 sts)
Rnds 1, 2 and 3 P1, k4, p1.

Rnd 4 P1, sl 2 sts to cn and hold to *back*, k2, k2 from cn, p1. Rep rnds 1–4 for right cable pat.

Left Cable Pattern
(worked in rnds over a panel of 6 sts)
Rnds 1, 2, and 3 P1, k4, p1.
Rnd 4 P1, sl 2 sts to cn and hold to *front*, k2, k2 from cn, p1. Rep rnds 1–4 for left cable pat.

Socks
(make 2)
Beg at the toe end of the sock, with waste yarn, cast on 14 (14, 16) sts. Divide sts onto 3 dpn with 3 (3, 4) sts on Needle 1, 4 sts on Needle 2 and 7 (7, 8) sts on Needle 3. The first two dpn hold sts for the top of the foot; 3rd dpn holds the sole sts. With working yarn, join to work in rnds, taking care not to twist sts, and pm to mark beg of rnd.
Foundation rnd 1 K1 tbl of each st around.
Foundation rnd 2 Knit.

Toe
Rnd 1 *Needle 1* Kfb, k to end of needle; *Needle 2* K to the last 2 sts, kfb, k1; *Needle 3* Kfb, k to the last 2 sts, kfb, k1—4 sts inc'd.
Rnd 2 Knit.
Rep these 2 rnds 5 (7, 8) times more—9 (11, 13) sts on Needle 1, 10 (12, 13) sts on Needle 2, and 19 (23, 26) sts on Needle 3.
Inc rnd *Needle 1* Kfb, k to end of needle; *Needle 2* K to the last 2 sts, kfb, k1; *Needle 3* Knit without inc's—10 (12, 14) sts on Needle 1, 11 (13, 14) sts on Needle 2, and 19 (23, 26) sts on Needle 3.

Size Small Only
Knit 1 rnd even, then rep the last inc rnd once more—42 (48, 54) sts: 11 (12, 14) sts on Needle 1, 12 (13, 14) sts on Needle 2, and 19 (23, 26) sts on Needle 3.

All Sizes
Begin cable patterns
Rnd 1 *Needle 1* K1, work right cable pat rnd 1 over 6 sts, k to end of needle; *Needle 2* K to the last 7 sts, work left cable rnd 1 over 6 sts, k1; *Needle 3* Knit.
Cont to work in established pat with cable insets until the piece measures (from beg of the toe) half the total length of the foot, ending with an odd-numbered pat rnd.

Gusset
Inc rnd 1 M1L, pm, work in pat to end of Needle 2, pm, M1R, k to end of rnd.
Rnd 2 Knit.
Inc rnd 3 K to marker, M1L, sl marker, work in pat to next marker, sl marker, M1R, k to end of rnd.
Rnd 4 Knit.

Cont to rep the last 2 rnds, always inc as established by M1L before the k1 that precedes the right cable pat and M1R after the k1 that follows the left cable pat, until there are 24 (25, 28) sts on Needle 1 and 25 (26, 28) sts on Needle 2—49 (51, 56) sts on Needles 1 and 2 for the instep sts and 19 (23, 26) sts for the sole.
Next (inc) rnd Rep inc rnd 3 on Needles 1 and 2 only, then transfer these 51 (53, 58) sts to a strand of waste yarn while working the heel.

Turn Heel
Working on the 19 (23, 26) sole sts from Needle 3 only, turn the heel by working back and forth in short rows as foll:
Short row 1 (RS) K to the last st on needle, w & t.
Short row 2 (WS) P to the last st on needle, w & t.
Short row 3 (RS) K to 1 st before the previous wrapped st, w & t.
Short row 4 (WS) P to 1 st before the previous wrapped st, w & t.
Rep short rows 3–4 until there are 7 (9, 10) unwrapped sts at the center and 6 (7, 8) wrapped sts on each side of these sts, end on a WS row. Then to close up the wraps, work as foll:
Transfer the instep sts back to 2 dpn to work along with the heel sts. Heel is worked back and forth, joining sole sts to top-of-foot sts at the end of each row.
Row 1 (RS) K the 7 (9, 10) heel sts, then k the next sts from heel, closing up the wraps on each st, then k2tog tbl the last st from heel with the first st from instep, turn.
Row 2 (WS) Sl 1, p the heel sts, closing up the wraps, then p2tog the last st from heel with the first st from instep, turn.
Row 3 (RS) Sl 1, k to the last st on heel, then k2tog tbl the last st from heel with the first st from instep, turn.
Row 4 (WS) Sl 1, p to the last st on heel, then p2tog tbl the last st from heel with the first st from instep, turn.
Rep rows 3 and 4 until all sts from heel have been joined to the instep and there are 19 (23, 26) sts once more on the 2 dpn for the top-of-foot sts. Then, cont to work all sts in pat in the previous established rnds for 9"/23cm, end with a cable rnd 4.
Next rnd *K1, p1, kfb; rep from * to the last 4 sts of 2nd dpn, kfb, then (k1, p1) to end of rnd.
Work 3 rnds more in k1, p1 rib. Bind off all sts as foll:
K1, *yo, p1, pass k1 over the yo, p1, k1, then pass both yo and p1 over the k1; rep from * around until all sts are bound off.

Note If the first sock was knit with the yarn from the inside of the ball, work 2nd sock beg with yarn from the outside of the ball.

Finishing
Remove the waste yarn from provisional cast-on and place sts on 2 needles—one needle for sole sts and one for top of foot. Holding needles parallel, use Kitchener st to weave the toe sts tog. Weave in ends and block to knitted measurements. ❖

Felted Tote

Felted Tote

Designed by Erica Schlueter

Four large mitered triangles are knit in quadrants and shaped using short rows. The fabric is then felted with measured abandon into this exquisite tote.

Skill Level
■■■□

Size
Instructions are written for one size.

Knitted Measurements
Before felting 18½"/47cm square
After felting 16½"/42cm square

Materials
■ 6 1¾oz/50g balls (each approx 110yd/100m) of Noro *Silk Garden* (silk/mohair/wool) in #301 Royal/Purple/Fuchsia/Lime (**4**)
■ One each size 8 (5mm) circular needle, 16"/40cm and 24"/60cm long, OR SIZE TO OBTAIN GAUGE
■ Size K/10½ (7mm) crochet hook
■ Waste yarn

Gauge
16 sts and 32 rows to 4"/10cm over garter st using size 8 (5mm) needles, *after* felting. TAKE TIME TO CHECK GAUGE.

Provisional Cast-on
Using waste yarn and crochet hook, chain the number of sts to cast on plus a few extra. Cut a tail and pull the tail through the last chain. With knitting needle and working yarn, pick up and knit the stated number of sts through the "purl bumps" on the back of the chain. To remove waste yarn chain, when instructed, pull out the tail from the last crochet stitch. Gently and slowly pull on the tail to unravel the crochet stitches, carefully placing each released knit stitch on the knitting needle.

3-Needle Bind-Off
1) With an even number of stitches on both needles, hold right sides of pieces parallel with tips in the same direction. Insert third needle knitwise into first st of each needle, and wrap yarn knitwise.
2) Knit these two sts together, and slip them off the needles. *Knit the next two sts together in the same manner.
3) Slip the first st on 3rd needle over 2nd st and off needle. Rep from * until all sts are bound off.

Short Row Wrap & Turn (w & t)
On RS row (on WS row)
1) Wyib (wyif), sl next st purlwise.
2) Move yarn between the needles to the front (back).
3) Sl the same st back to LH needle, turn work. One st is wrapped.
4) When working the wrapped st, insert RH needle under the wrap and work it tog with the corresponding st on needle.

Note
The diagram shows the method of working each mitered square that makes up the front and back of the tote.

Back
With shorter circular needle, using the provisional cast-on method and waste yarn, cast on 39 sts. Change to working yarn.
Short row 1 (WS) K37, w & t.
Short row 2 (RS) K to end of row.
Short row 3 K36, w & t.
Short row 4 K to end of row.
Short row 5 K to 1 st *less* than previous WS short row, w & t.
Short row 6 K to end of row on this and all RS short rows.
Short row 7–67 (WS) Rep short row 5.
Short row 68 (RS) K5.
The first ½ quadrant is completed.

Second ½ Quadrant
Short row 1 (WS) K5, close up the wrap with the next st, turn.

Short row 2 (RS) K to end of row.
Short row 3 (WS) K6, close up the wrap with the next st, turn.
Short row 4 K to end of row.
Short row 5 K to 1 st *more* than the previous short row, then close up the wrap with the next st, turn. Rep these 2 rows until all 39 sts are worked on the last RS row. The second ½ quadrant is completed.

Work ½ quadrants 3 and 4, 5 and 6, then 7 and 8 in same way. Leave 39 sts on hold. Finish the square by first removing the waste yarn from the provisional cast-on. Then, with sts from the last quadrant and the cast-on edge sts on 2 needles held parallel with the RS of pieces tog, work a 3-needle bind-off on the *WS* of tote to close up the square.

Front
Work same as back.

Straps
(make 2)
Cast on 6 sts and work in garter st for 20"/51cm (or desired length). Bind off.

Finishing
Using the mattress st from the RS, sew three sides of tote tog, leaving approx 1½"/4cm open at each top edge. Baste each strap to top edge approx 3½"/9cm in from each seam edge and with an overlap of approx 1½"/4cm from each strap end placed to the WS (for reinforcement of the strap). Carefully sew in place on the WS, sewing through fabric several times for extra reinforcement.

Felting
Place finished piece in lingerie bag or pillow case with old towels (colors may run in the hot water). Place the bag in a top-loading washing machine and wash with soap and hot water. Stop and check the bag from time to time. If you like the size of the bag the last time you check it, remove from the washer rinse; if you want the bag more tightly felted, let it go through the rinse cycle in the machine. Be aware that, if it is a cold rinse cycle, the bag may shrink more than before. After rinsing, place in 1 gallon of water with a tablespoon of white vinegar for 10 minutes, then rinse. Depending on the length of wash cycle, it may take a few washings to felt the bag tightly. Wrap in towel and press out as much water as possible. Block into desired shape. Due to the nature of the yarn, the open edge may be uneven after felting. Blocking may help to straighten the edge. ❖

Felted Measurements

16½"

16½"

Begin here →

Direction of work

2   3
1   4
8   5
7   6

Bamboo-Stitch Shoulder Wrap

Bamboo-Stitch Shoulder Wrap

Designed by Bea Naretto

The stranded effect of the bamboo stitch pattern plays fast and loose with an extra-large needle size in this drapey shoulder wrap.

Skill Level
■■□□

Size
Instructions are written for one size.

Knitted Measurements
Circumference 48"/122cm
Height 19"/48cm

Materials
■ 6 1¾oz/50g balls (each approx 110yd/100m) of *Noro Silk Garden* (silk/mohair/wool) in #366 Violet/Black/Sky Blue/Pink
■ One each sizes 10½ and 15 (6.5 and 10 mm) circular needle, 40"/100cm long, OR SIZE TO OBTAIN GAUGE

Gauge
14 sts and 24 rnds to 4"/10cm over bamboo pat st using larger needle. TAKE TIME TO CHECK GAUGE.

Bamboo Pattern Stitch
(multiple of 6 sts)
Rnd 1 Knit.
Rnd 2 *Sl 1, k1 into the running thread between the sl st and the next st, sl 1, k1, then with tip of LH needle, pass the first sl st over the other 3 sts (for one *bamboo st*); rep from * to end.
Rnd 3 Knit.
Rnd 4 K2, *work one bamboo st; rep from * around, end k1.
Rnd 5 Knit.
Rnd 6 K1, *work 1 bamboo st; rep from *, end k2.
Rep rnds 1–6 for bamboo pat st.

Wrap
With smaller needle, cast on 168 sts. Join to work in rnds, taking care not to twist sts on needle and pm to mark beg of rnd.
Rnd 1 *K3, p3; rep from * around.
Rep rnd 1 for 5 rnds more.
Begin Bamboo Pattern Stitch
Change to larger needle and work in bamboo pat st, rep rnds 1–6, until piece measures 18"/45.5cm from beg, end with a knit rnd. Change to smaller needle.
Next rnd *K3, p3; rep from * around.
Rep this rnd for 4 rnds more. Bind off in rib.

Finishing
Block finished piece to measurements. ❖

Cabled Scarf

Cabled Scarf

Designed by Wei Wilkins

This extra-wide scarf features swirling cables and a deep fringe, perfectly cozy for a cold winter's day.

Skill Level
■■■□

Size
Instructions are written for one size.

Knitted Measurements
Length (excluding fringe) 60"/152cm
Width 10½"/26.5cm

Materials
- 6 1¾oz/50g balls (each approx 137yd/125m) of Noro *Silk Garden Lite* (silk/mohair/wool) in #2094 Green/Orange/Salmon/Brown (3)
- One pair each sizes 6 and 8 (4 and 5mm) needles, OR SIZE TO OBTAIN GAUGE
- Size H/8 (5mm) crochet hook
- Cable needle (cn)

Stitch Glossary
4-st RPC Sl 2 sts to cn and hold to *back*, k2, p2 from cn.
4-st LPC Sl 2 sts to cn and hold to *front*, p2, k2 from cn.
5-st RPC Sl 3 sts to cn and hold to *back*, k2, then sl the last st from cn back to LH needle and p this st, then k2 from cn.
5-st RPC (dec 2) Sl 3 sts to cn and hold to *back*, k2tog, k1, then p1, k1 from cn and work ssk with the last st from cn and next st on LH needle.
Inc 7 In this st work (k1, yo, k1, yo, k1, yo, k1)—7 sts made from 1 st.

Gauge
23 sts and 23 rows to 4"/10cm over chart pat using larger needles.
TAKE TIME TO CHECK GAUGE.

Scarf
With smaller needles, cast on 61 sts.
Set-up row 1 (RS) Knit.
Change to larger needles.
Set-up row 2 (WS) K3 (edge sts), p2, k2, p2, k1, p2, k2, p2, [p3, k2, p2, k1, p2, k2, p2] 3 times, end k3 (edge sts).

Begin Chart Pattern
Row 1 (RS) K3 (edge sts), working row 1 of chart, work the 14-st rep 3 times, work sts 15–27 of chart once, k3 (edge sts). Cont to foll chart in this way (with the k3 edge sts worked at beg and end of every row), working the 24-row rep until piece measures approx 60"/152cm from beg, ending with row 7 of chart.
Note When working the final rep of rows 5–7 of the chart, do *not* work the inset chart, but work inset-chart sts as k1 instead.
Change to smaller needles and knit 1 row. Bind off.

Finishing
Block finished piece to measurements. Mark for 20 fringes on each end of scarf. Wrap yarn around a 7½"/19cm piece of cardboard 8 times and cut at one end. Using crochet hook, pull the loop at the fringe fold through one edge of scarf, then pull the ends through the loop and tighten with the knot on the RS. Trim all fringe evenly. ❖

CABLE CHART

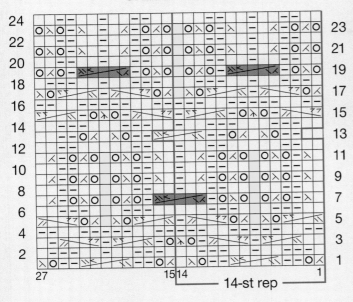

24   23
22   21
20   19
18   17
16   15
14   13
12   11
10   9
8   7
6   5
4   3
2   1

27   15 14   1

14-st rep

INSET CHART

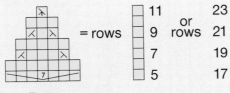

= rows   11   or   23
         9   rows   21
         7   19
         5   17

7 sts

STITCH KEY

☐ k on RS, p on WS

⊟ p on RS, k on WS

⊙ yo

◩ k2tog

◪ ssk

▣ SK2P

4-st RPC

4-st LPC

5-st RPC

5-st RPC (dec 2)

Inc 7

Modular Pieced Cape

Modular Pieced Cape

Designed by Dorcas Lavery

A fun, fascinating series of rectangles, triangles and squares comes together seamlessly in this very wearable cape design.

Skill Level
■■■■

Size
Instructions are written for one size.

Knitted Measurements
Back width 33"/84 cm
Length (at center back) 28"/71 cm
Length (at front) 16"/40.5 cm

Materials
■ 8 1¾oz/50g balls (each approx 110yd/100m) Noro *Silk Garden* (silk/mohair/wool) in #389 Orange/Lilac/Purple/Pink (④)
■ One size 8 (5mm) circular needle, 24"/60cm long, OR SIZE TO OBTAIN GAUGE
■ Stitch markers
■ One 1⅜"/34mm button

Gauge
17 sts and 34 rows to 4"/10cm over garter st stripe pat using size 8 (5mm) needle. TAKE TIME TO CHECK GAUGE.

Stitch Glossary
SK2P at marker Sl 2 sts, remove marker, slip last st back to LH needle, k2tog, psso, replace marker—2 sts dec'd.

Notes
1) Each piece is knit in garter stitch using 1 ball for 2 rows, then using a separate ball for 2 rows. This 2-color striping is worked throughout. Use a removable stitch marker or safety pin to mark the RS.
2) Cape is constructed as foll: Knit left side in one piece, blocks 1–6. Knit right side in one piece, blocks 7–12. Join the two side pieces together by knitting blocks 13 and 14, then follow the instructions to finish off the neck opening. Knit the center front bands onto block 9 and block 3. Tack blocks 4 and 5 together under the arms. Tack blocks 10 and 11 together under the arms. Seam block 6 and block 12 together along the center.
3) Diagram can be found on page 139.

Left Side
Block 1
Row 1 With ball 1, cast on 30 sts, pm, cast on 60 sts, pm, cast on 30 sts—120 sts.
Row 2 SKP, k to the marker, sl marker, p1, k to the next marker, sl marker, p1, k to end—119 sts.
Row 3 (RS) With ball 2, k to 2 sts before marker, SK2P at marker, k to 2 sts before marker, SK2P at marker, k to end.
Row 4 K to marker, sl marker, p1, k to next marker, sl marker, p1, k to end.
Rows 5 and 6 With ball 1, rep rows 3 and 4.
Rep the last 4 rows until 7 sts rem.
Next row (RS) Rep row 3, removing markers—3 sts.
Last row (WS) P3tog—1 st.

Block 2
With 1 st rem on the needle, cast on 29 sts to end of needle—30 sts.
Row 1 K30, pm, then with the RS of the block facing (using the garter st bumps), pick up and k 30 sts along top of block 1, cast on 30 more sts, pm, cast on 30 sts—120 sts.
Beg with row 2, work as for block 1.

Block 3
With the 1 st rem on needle from block 2, work as for block 2, picking up sts along top of block 2, then fasten off the final st.

Triangle Block 4
Row 1 From the RS with ball 1, pick up and k 30 sts along lower edge of block 3, pm, pick up and k 30 sts along side edge of block 2.
Row 2 (WS) SKP, k to marker, sl marker, p1, k to end.
Row 3 (RS) With ball 2, k to 2 sts before marker, SK2P at marker, k to end.
Rep rows 2–3 in the stripe pat until 4 sts rem, end with (WS) row 2.
Last row (RS) Sl 1, k3tog, psso. Fasten off last st.

Triangle Block 5
Work as for triangle block 4, between blocks 2 and 1.

Triangle Block 6
Row 1 From the RS, pick up and k 30 sts along the inside edge of block 1, pm, pick up and k 30 sts along the lower edge of block 2—60 sts.
Row 2 (WS) SKP, k to marker, sl marker, p1, k to last 2 sts, k2tog.
Row 3 (RS) SKP, k to 2 sts before marker, SK2P at marker, k to last 2 sts, k2tog.
Rep rows 2–3 until 4 sts rem.
Next row SK2P, k1.
Last row P3tog and fasten off last st.

Right Side
Block 7
Work as for block 1, then fasten off last st and cut yarn.

Block 8
Cast on 30 sts, pm, cast on 30 more sts, pick up and k 30 sts in side of (to the center of) block 7, pm, cast on 30 more sts—120 sts. Beg with row 2, work as for block 1. Fasten off last st.

Block 9
Work as for block 8, picking up sts along side of (to the center of) block 8.

Triangle Block 10
Work as for triangle block 4, between blocks 8 and 9.

Triangle Block 11
Work as for triangle block 4, between blocks 7 and 8.

Triangle Block 12
Work as for triangle block 6, between blocks 7 and 8.

Join the Right and Left Sides
Square Block 13
Row 1 From the RS, pick up and k 30 sts along the inside edge of block 1, pm, pick up and k 30 sts along the inside edge of block 7—60 sts.
Row 2 (WS) SKP, k to marker, sl marker, p1, k to end.
Row 3 (RS) K to 2 sts before marker, SK2P at marker, k to end.
Row 4 K to marker, sl marker, p1, k to end. Rep the last 2 rows until 3 sts rem.
Last row P3tog, fasten off and cut yarn.

Triangle Block 14
Work as for triangle block 4, between blocks 2 and 8.

Finishing
Seam tog triangle blocks 6 and 12 to complete the piece.

Neck Trim
Row 1 With ball 1, pick up and k 31 sts along neck edge of block 9, pm, pick up and k 33 sts along open neck edge of block 14, pm, pick up and k 31 sts along neck edge of block 3—95 sts.
Cont with 2 rows from ball 1 and 2 as before, work as foll:
Row 2 (WS) K to marker, sl marker, p1, k to next marker, sl marker, p1, k to end.
Row 3 (RS) [K to 2 sts before marker, SK2P at marker] twice, k to end.
Rep the last 2 rows 4 times more—75 sts. Bind off all sts.

Left Front Border
Row 1 From the RS, pick up and k 68 sts along the center front edge of block 3. Cont with 2 rows from ball 1 and 2 rows from ball 2 as before, work as foll:
Row 2 *K1, p1; rep from * to end.
Row 3 K the purl and p the knit sts.
Rep row 3 for seed st pat for 6 rows more. Bind off in pat.

Right Front Border
Work as for left front border for 5 rows.
Buttonhole row (RS) Work 61 sts in seed st, bind off 3 sts, work to end. On next row, cast on 3 sts over the bound-off sts. Complete as for left front border. Tack together blocks 4 and 5, and blocks 10 and 11, for the underarms. Sew on button opposite buttonhole. ✤

Linen Stitch Scarf

Linen Stitch Scarf

Designed by Sarah Thieneman

Classic, reversible linen stitch pairs with a multicolor seamless fringe in this tailored basic.

Skill Level
■■☐☐

Size
Instructions are written for one size.

Knitted Measurements
Length (excluding fringe) 68"/172.5cm
Width 6¼"/16cm

Materials
■ 3 1¾oz/50g balls (each approx 110yd/100m) each of *Noro Silk Garden* each in #395 Purple/Black/Blue/Violet (A) and #301 Royal/Purple/Fuchsia/Lime (B) (④)
■ One size 9 (5.5mm) circular needle, 40"/100cm long, OR SIZE TO OBTAIN GAUGE

Gauge
20 sts and 40 rows to 4"/10cm over linen stitch pat (before blocking) using size 9 (5.5mm) needle. TAKE TIME TO CHECK GAUGE.

Linen Stitch Pattern
(odd number of sts)
Row 1 (RS) K1, *k1, sl 1 purlwise wyif, take yarn to back; rep from *, end k2.
Row 2 (WS) K1, sl 1 purlwise wyib, *take yarn to front, p1, sl 1 purlwise wyib; rep from *, end k1.

Note
Linen stitch creates a dense, stable fabric that will open up slightly during steam blocking and finish to the knitted measurements as stated.

Scarf
Leaving at least a 3"/7.5cm end, with color A, cast on 305 sts.
Row 1 (RS) With A, work row 1 of linen stitch pattern. Cut A, leaving at least a 3"/7.5cm end.
Row 2 (WS) Attach A, leaving at least a 3"/7.5cm end, and work row 2 of linen stitch pattern. Cut A, leaving at least a 3"/7.5cm end.
Rows 3–6 Rep rows 1 and 2 twice.
Row 7 Attach B, leaving at least a 3"/7.5cm end, and work row 1 of linen stitch pattern. Cut B, leaving at least a 3"/7.5cm end.
Row 8 Attach B, leaving at least a 3"/7.5cm end, and work row 2 of linen stitch pattern. Cut B, leaving at least a 3"/7.5cm end.
Rows 9–12 Rep rows 7 and 8 twice.
Rep these 12 rows until there are a total of 9 color stripes or 54 rows. (The last 6 rows will be worked in color A.)
Attach A, leaving at least a 3"/7.5cm end, and bind off evenly with A, leaving at least a 3"/7.5cm end.

Finishing
Trim fringe at each end to measure evenly. Block scarf to knitted measurements. ❖

Hyacinth Stitch Shawl

Hyacinth Stitch Shawl

Designed by Linda Medina

Worked in earthy woodland shades, the hyacinth stitch pattern creates a lush texture for this wide triangular shawl.

Skill Level
■ ■ ■ □

Size
Instructions are written for one size.

Knitted Measurements
Wingspan 66"/168cm
Height 19"/48cm

Materials
- 4 1¾oz/50g balls (each approx 137yd/125m) of Noro *Silk Garden Lite* (silk/mohair/lambswool) in #2084 Black/Grey/Purple/Brown (3)
- One size 8 (5mm) circular needle, 40"/150cm long, OR SIZE TO OBTAIN GAUGE
- Two size 8 (5mm) double-pointed needles (dpn)

Stitch Glossary
P5tog To make the p5tog easier, it can be worked as foll: wyif, sl next 4 sts one at a time purlwise, then p next st and lift each slipped st over the last p st, one at a.time—4 sts dec'd.

Gauge
20 sts and 18 rows to 4"/10cm over hyacinth stitch pat using size 8 (5mm) needles. TAKE TIME TO CHECK GAUGE.

Hyacinth Stitch Pattern
(multiple of 6 sts plus 2)
Cast on sts and knit one set-up row.
Row 1 (WS) K1,*p5tog, (k1,p1, k1, p1, k1) in next st; rep from * to last st, end k1.
Row 2 (RS) K1, p to last st, k1.
Row 3 K1, *(k1, p1, k1, p1, k1) in next st, p5tog; rep from * to last st, end k1.
Row 4 K1, p to last st, k1.
Row 5 K1, *k next st, wrapping yarn twice around needle; rep from * to last st, end k1.
Row 6 K1, *k next st, letting the extra wrap drop from needle; rep from * to last st, end k1.
Rep rows 1–6 for hyacinth stitch pattern.

Note
Markers are placed on the set-up row and moved every row to delineate the edge sts from the pat sts. As sts are inc'd, it is helpful to add new markers to mark each new set of 6-st pats. Work any inc'd sts outside of these reps in St st (k on the RS, p on the WS).

Shawl
With circular needle, loosely cast on 12 sts.
Set-up row (WS) Kfb, k to last st, kfb—14 sts.
Row 1 (RS) Kfb, yo, p to last st, yo, kfb—4 sts inc'd.
Row 2 (WS) Kfb, k1, (k1, p1, k1, p1, k1) in next st; *p5tog, (k1, p1, k1, p1, k1) in next st; rep from * to last 3 sts, k2, kfb—2 sts inc'd.
Row 3 Rep row 1.
Row 4 Kfb, k4, p5tog, *(k1, p1, k1, p1, k1) in next st, p5tog; rep from * to last 6 sts, k5, kfb.
Row 5 Rep row 1.
Row 6 Kfb, k2, *k, wrapping yarn around needle twice; rep from * to last 3 sts, k2, kfb.
Row 7 Kfb, yo, p3, *k, dropping extra wrap from needle; rep from * to last 4 sts, p3, yo, kfb.
Row 8 Kfb, k5, *p5tog, (k1, p1, k1, p1, k1) in next st; rep from * to last 6 sts, k5, kfb.
Row 9 Rep row 1.
Row 10 Kfb, k2, *(k1, p1, k1, p1, k1) in next st, p5tog; rep from * to last 3 sts, k2, kfb.
Row 11 Rep row 1.
Row 12 Kfb, k5, *k, wrapping yarn around needle twice; rep from * to last 6 sts, k5, kfb.

Row 13 Kfb, yo, p6, *k, dropping extra wrap from needle; rep from * to last 7 sts, p6, yo, kfb.

Row 14 Kfb, k2, *p5tog, (k1, p1, k1, p1, k1) in next st; rep from * to last 3 sts, k2, kfb.

Row 15 Rep row 1.

Row 16 Kfb, k5, *(k1, p1, k1, p1, k1) in next st, p5tog; rep from * to last 6 sts, k5, kfb.

Row 17 Rep row 1.

Row 18 Rep row 6.

Row 19 Rep row 7.

Rows 20–55 Rep (rows 8–19) 3 times more—180 sts.

Rows 56–60 Rep rows 8–12—194 sts.

Row 61 Rep row 13.

Row 62 Cast on 6 sts, rep row 14.

Row 63 Cast on 6 sts, rep row 1—216 sts.

Row 64 Rep row 16.

Row 65 Rep row 1.

Row 66 Cast on 6 sts, rep row 6.

Row 67 Cast on 6 sts, rep row 7—240 sts.

Row 68 Rep row 8.

Row 69 Rep row 1.

Row 70 Cast on 6 sts, rep row 10.

Row 71 Cast on 6 sts, rep row 1.

Row 72 Rep row 12—262 sts.

Row 73 Rep row 13.

Row 74 Cast on 6 sts, rep row 14.

Row 75 Cast on 6 sts, rep row 1.

Row 76 Cast on 6 sts, rep row 16.

Row 77 Cast on 6 sts, rep row 1.

Row 78 Cast on 6 sts, rep row 6.

Row 79 Cast on 6 sts, kfb, yo, p9, *k next st, letting the extra wrap drop from needle; rep from * to last 4 sts, p3, yo, kfb.

Row 80 Cast on 6 sts, rep row 8.

Row 81 Cast on 6 sts, rep row 1—336 sts.

Row 82 Purl. Bind off loosely knitwise.

Finishing

Weave in ends and block shawl to measurements.

Picot Edging

Using 2 dpn, make a slip knot and place on 1 dpn. *Using the cable cast-on, cast on 2 more sts—3 sts on needle. Bind off 2 sts—1 st rem on needle. Sl this st to LH needle—1 picot made.

Rep from * until there are 164 picots. Ensure that this picot edge fits the entire outer edge of the triangle, then cont to work the edging as foll: Using circular needle, do not turn work and then, working into the straight edge of the picots, *yo, pick up and k1 st in loop of the picot; rep from * to end—328 sts. Knit 4 rows. Bind off. Using mattress st, graft the edging to the outer edge of the triangle from the RS. ✤

Autumn Leaves Shawl

Autumn Leaves Shawl

Designed by Anna Stoklosa

Falling leaves and the golden hues of autumn are the inspiration for this free-form shawl, composed of individual leaves in a one-of-a-kind design.

Skill Level
■■■□

Size
Instructions are written for one size.

Knitted Measurements
Wingspan 52"/132cm
Height 34"/86cm
Large leaf approx 8"/20.5cm square
Medium leaf approx 6"/15cm x 7"/18cm
Small leaf approx 5"/12.5cm x 6"/15cm

Materials
■ 4 3½oz/100g balls (each approx 328yd/300m) of Noro *Silk Garden Sock* (wool/silk/polyamide/mohair) in #421 Desert Oranges/Green (2)
■ One pair size 6 (4mm) needles, OR SIZE TO OBTAIN GAUGE
■ Stitch holders or waste yarn

Gauge
18 sts and 23 rows to 4"/10cm over St st using size 6 (4mm) needles. TAKE TIME TO CHECK GAUGE.

Note
The shawl size is figured based on working a total of 54 leaves, with 18 leaves in each of the 3 leaf sizes. The leaves are laid out in a random fashion.

Large Leaf
(make 18)
Cast on 7 sts.
Row 1 (WS) Purl.
Row 2 (RS) Sl 1, [yo, k1] 6 times—13 sts.
Rows 3, 5, 7, 9 and 11 Purl.
Row 4 Sl 1, [yo, k1] 12 times—25 sts.
Row 6 Sl 1, [k3, yo, k1, yo] 5 times, k4—35 sts.
Row 8 Sl 1, k4, [yo, k1, yo, k5] 5 times—45 sts.
Row 10 Sl 1, k5, [yo, k1, yo, k2, k3tog, k2] 4 times, yo, k1, yo, k6—47 sts.
Row 12 K2tog, k5, yo, k1, yo, k7, [yo, k1, yo, k2, k3tog, k2] twice, yo, k1, yo, k7, yo, k1, yo, k5, k2tog—51 sts.
Row 13 (WS) P2tog, p to the last 2 sts, p2tog—49 sts.
Row 14 K2tog, k4, yo, k1, yo, k9, [yo, k1, yo, k7] twice, yo, k1, yo, k9, yo, k1, yo, k4, k2tog—57 sts.
Leaf Tip 1
Row 1 (WS) P2tog, p11 (12 sts on RH needle); turn work, leaving the rem sts on hold.
Row 2 (RS) Bind off 2 sts, k3 (4 sts on RH needle), yo, k1, yo, k3, k2tog—11 sts.
Rows 3, 5, 7 and 9 P2tog, p to the last 2 sts, p2tog.
Row 4 K2tog, k2, yo, k1, yo, k2, k2tog—9 sts.
Row 6 K2tog, k1, yo, k1, yo, k1, k2tog—7 sts.
Row 8 K2tog, yo, k1, yo, k2tog—5 sts.
Row 10 K3tog. Fasten off last st, leaving a long end for finishing.
Leaf Tip 2
Rejoin yarn from the WS to the 44 sts on hold and work as foll:
Row 1 (WS) P to the last 13 sts and leave these worked sts on hold, then p2tog, p9, p2tog.
Row 2 (RS) K2tog, k3, yo, k1, yo, k3, k2tog (11 sts on RH needle); turn work, leaving the rem 31 sts on hold.
Rows 3–10 Work same as for leaf tip 1.
Center Section
Rejoin yarn from the RS to the 31 sts on hold and work as foll:
Row 1 (RS) K5, [yo, k1, yo, k9] twice, yo, k1, yo, k5—37 sts.
Rows 2 and 4 Purl.

Row 3 Sl 1, k5, [yo, k1, yo, k11] twice, yo, k1, yo, k6—43 sts.

Row 5 (RS) Sl 1, k6, [yo, k1, yo, k13] twice, yo, k1, yo, k7—49 sts.

Leaf Tip 3

Row 1 (WS) Bind off 3 sts, purl until there are 13 sts on RH needle; turn, leaving the rem sts on hold.

Row 2 (RS) Bind off 3 sts, k until there are 4 sts on RH needle, yo, k1, yo, k3, k2tog—11 sts.

Rows 3–10 Work same as for leaf tip 1.

Leaf Tip 4

Rejoin yarn from the WS to the 33 sts on hold and work as foll:

Row 1 (WS) P until there are 17 sts on RH needle. Sl these 17 sts to a st holder for the center. With a 2nd ball of yarn, bind off 2 sts, p to end.

Row 2 (RS) Bind off 4 sts, k until there are 4 sts on RH needle, yo, k1, yo, k3, k2tog—11 sts.

Rows 3–10 Work same as for leaf tip 1.

Leaf Tip 5

Return to the sts on hold for the center and, with dropped yarn, work as foll:

Row 1 (RS) K8, yo, k1, yo, k8—19 sts.

Rows 2 and 4 Purl.

Row 3 Sl 1, k8, yo, k1, yo, k9—21 sts.

Row 5 Sl 1, k9, yo, k1, yo, k10—23 sts.

Row 6 Bind off 6 sts, p to end—17 sts.

Row 7 Bind off 7 sts, k until there are 4 sts on RH needle, yo, k1, yo, k3, k2tog—11 sts.

Next 8 rows Work same as for rows 3–10 of leaf tip 1.

Medium Leaf

(make 18)

Cast on 7 sts and work rows 1–10 same as for Large leaf—47 sts.

Next row Bind off 2 sts, purl to end—45 sts.

Next row Bind off 2 sts, sl st on RH needle back to LH needle and k2tog, k3, yo, k1, yo, k7, [yo, k1, yo, k2, k3tog, k2] twice, yo, k1, yo, k7, yo, k1, yo, k3, k2tog—47 sts.

Leaf Tip 1

Row 1 (WS) P2tog, p8 (9 sts on RH needle); turn work, leaving the rem sts on hold.

Next 7 rows Work same as for leaf tip 1 rows 4–10.

Leaf Tip 2

Rejoin yarn from the WS to the 37 sts on hold and work as foll:

Row 1 (WS) P to the last 11 sts, p2tog, p7, p2tog—9 sts.

Next 7 rows Work same as for leaf tip 1 rows 4–10.

Center Section

Rejoin yarn from the RS to the 26 sts on hold and work as foll:

Row 1 (RS) K4, [yo, k1, yo, k7] twice, yo, k1, yo, k5—32 sts.

Row 2 Purl.

Row 3 Sl 1, k4, [yo, k1, yo, k9] twice, yo, k1, yo, k6—38 sts.

Leaf Tip 3

Row 1 (WS) Bind off 3 sts, purl until there are 10 sts on RH needle; turn work, leaving the rem sts on hold.

Row 2 (RS) Bind off 2 sts, k until there are 3 sts on RH needle, yo, k1, yo, k2, k2tog—9 sts.

Next 6 rows Work same as for leaf tip 1 rows 5–10.

Leaf Tip 4

Rejoin yarn from the WS to the 25 sts on hold and work as foll:

Row 1 (WS) P13, place these sts on a st holder, bind off 1 st, p to end.

Row 2 (RS) Bind off 3 sts, k until there are 3 sts on RH needle, yo, k1, yo, k2, k2tog—9 sts. Complete as for leaf tip 3.

Leaf Tip 5

Return to the sts on holder, rejoin yarn from the RS and work as foll:

Row 1 (RS) K6, yo, k1, yo, k6—15 sts.

Rows 2 and 4 Purl.

Row 3 Sl 1, k6, yo, k1, yo, k7—17 sts.

Row 5 Sl 1, k7, yo, k1, yo, k8—19 sts.

Row 6 Bind off 4 sts, p to end.

Row 7 Bind off 5 sts, k until there are 4 sts on RH needle, yo, k1, yo, k3, k2tog—11 sts.

Next 8 rows Work as for rows 3–10 of leaf tip 1.

Small Leaf

(make 18)

Cast on 7 sts and work rows 1–7 same as for Large leaf—35 sts.

Row 8 (RS) K2tog, k3, [yo, k1, yo, k1, k3tog, k1] 4 times, yo, k1, yo, k3, k2tog.

Row 9 P2tog, p to last 2 sts, p2tog—33 sts.

Row 10 K2tog, k2, yo, k1, yo, k5, [yo, k1, yo, k1, k3tog, k1] twice, yo, k1, yo, k5, yo, k1, yo, k2, k2tog—37 sts.

Leaf Tip 1

Row 1 (WS) P2tog, p7—8 sts; turn work, leaving rem sts on hold.

Row 2 (RS) Bind off 2 sts, k until there are 2 sts on RH needle, [yo, k1] twice, k2tog—7 sts.

Row 3 P2tog, p3, p2tog—5 sts.

Row 4 K2tog, yo, k1, yo, k2tog.

Row 5 P2tog, p1, p2tog—3 sts.

Row 6 K3tog. Fasten off, leaving a long end for finishing.

Leaf Tip 2

Rejoin yarn from the WS to the 28 sts on hold and work as foll:

Row 1 (WS) P to the last 9 sts, p2tog, p5, p2tog.

Row 2 (RS) K2tog, k1, [yo, k1] twice, k2tog, turn work—7 sts. Complete as for previous leaf tips.

Center Section

Rejoin yarn from the RS to the 19 sts on hold and work as foll:

Row 1 (RS) K3, [yo, k1, yo, k5] twice, yo, k1, yo, k3—25 sts.

Row 3 Sl 1, k3, [yo, k1, yo, k7] twice, yo, k1, yo, k4—31 sts.

Leaf Tip 3

Row 1 (WS) P2tog, p8, turn work—9 sts. Complete as for previous leaf tips.

Leaf Tip 4

Rejoin yarn from the WS to the 21 sts on hold and work as foll:

Row 1 (WS) P to the last 10 sts on needle, p8, p2tog—9 sts. With center sts on hold, complete as for previous leaf tips.

Leaf Tip 5

Return to the sts on hold for the center and join yarn from the RS, work as foll:

Row 1 (RS) K5, yo, k1, yo, k5—13 sts.

Rows 2 and 4 Purl.

Row 3 Sl 1, k5, yo, k1, yo, k6—15 sts.

Row 5 Bind off 3 sts, k until there are 4 sts on RH needle, yo, k1, yo, k7—14 sts.

Row 6 Bind off 4 sts, p to last 2 sts, p2tog—9 sts. Complete as for previous leaf tips.

Finishing

Do not block the leaves, to retain the organic nature of the finished piece. To begin the triangular shape of the shawl, overlap 7 large leaves to make the center of the shawl, and sew the overlapped leaves tog (see photo for inspiration). Lay out all the other leaves as desired on each side of this center line of leaves and sew together. ❧

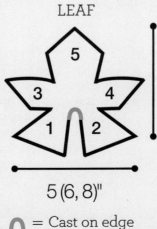

LEAF

5 (6, 8)"

⌒ = Cast on edge

Two-Color Tweed Hat

Two-Color Tweed Hat

Designed by Betty Balcomb

With the solid color forming a grid and the multi-color creating subtle seeded fill-ins, this tweedy slouchy hat sports an i-cord pull top.

Skill Level
■ ■ ☐ ☐

Size
Instructions are written for one size.

Knitted Measurements
Circumference 20"/51cm
Height 9"/23cm

Materials
- 1 1¾oz/50g ball (each approx 110yd/100m) of Noro *Silk Garden Solo* (silk/mohair/wool) in #3 Royal (A) (4)
- 1 1¾oz/50g ball (each approx 110yd/100m) of Noro *Silk Garden* (silk/mohair/wool) of #393 Red/Black/Orange/Purple/Green (B) (4)
- One each sizes 8 and 10 (5 and 6mm) circular needle, 16"/40cm long, OR SIZE TO OBTAIN GAUGE
- One set (5) size 10 (6mm) double-pointed needles (dpn)
- Stitch marker

Gauge
17 sts and 34 rnds to 4"/10cm over tweed pat st using larger needle. TAKE TIME TO CHECK GAUGE.

Tweed Pattern Stitch
(even number of sts)
Rnd 1 With A, knit.
Rnd 2 With A, purl.
Rnd 3 With B, *k1, sl 1 purlwise wyib; rep from * around.
Rnd 4 With B, *p1, take yarn to back and sl 1 purlwise wyib, take yarn to front; rep from * around, ending the last rep wyib.
Rep rows 1–4 for tweed pat st.

Note
When working with B, if there is not sufficient color contrast to the solid A color, simply cut out the segment until a contrast area of the color is reached and rejoin B at that point.

Hat
With smaller needle and A, cast on 84 sts. Join to work in rnds, taking care not to twist sts on needle, and pm to mark beg of rnd. Work in k2, p2 rib as foll:
Next rnd *K2, p2; rep from * around.
Work 7 more rnds of k2, p2 rib. Change to larger needle.
Begin Tweed Pattern Stitch
Beg with rnd 1, work in tweed pat st, rep rnds 1–4 until piece measures approx 8"/20.5cm from beg, ending with pat row 1.

Crown Shaping
Note Change to dpn (dividing sts evenly over 4 needles) when there are too few sts to fit comfortably on circular needle.
Dec rnd 1 With A, [p5, p2tog] 12 times—72 sts.
Work 3 rnds even.
Dec rnd 2 With A, p2, [p2tog, p4] 11 times, end p2tog, p2—60 sts.
Work 3 rnds even.
Dec rnd 3 With A, [p3, p2tog] 12 times—48 sts.
Work 3 rnds even.
Dec rnd 4 With A, p1, [p2tog, p2] 11 times, end p2tog, p1—36 sts.
Work 3 rnds even.
Dec rnd 5 With A, [p2tog, p1] 12 times—24 sts.
Work 3 rnds even.
Dec rnd 6 [P2tog] 12 times—12 sts.
Last rnd [K2tog] 6 times—6 sts.

I-cord Top
Slip all 6 sts to one dpn.
***Next rnd (RS)** K6, do *not* turn. Slide sts back to opposite end of needle to work next rnd from RS. Rep from * for approx 1"/2.5cm. Bind off.

Finishing
Weave in ends and block hat to knitted measurements. ❖

Graphic Triangles Cowl

Graphic Triangles Cowl

Designed by Cheryl Murray

Bold contrasting hues march across a background of beiges, then line up in crisp triangles on this closely knit cowl.

Skill Level
■ ■ □ □

Size
Instructions are written for one size.

Knitted Measurements
Depth 8½"/21.5cm
Circumference (bottom edge) 26"/66cm
Circumference (top edge) 24"/61cm

Materials
■ 1 3½oz/100 g ball (each approx 328yd/300m) of Noro *Silk Garden Sock* (wool/silk/polyamide/mohair) each in #407 Brown/Purple/White/Green (A) and #269 Cream/Tan/Grey (B) **2**
■ One each sizes 4 and 5 (3.5 and 3.75mm) circular needles, 24"/60cm long, OR SIZE TO OBTAIN GAUGE
■ Stitch marker

Gauge
24 sts and 32 rows/rnds to 4"/10cm over St st and chart pat using larger needle. TAKE TIME TO CHECK GAUGE.

Note
When working color pat foll chart, strand color not in use *loosely* across back of work, then twist yarns tog at the color change to avoid holes in work.

Cowl
With larger needle and A, cast on 144 sts. Join to work in rnds, taking care not to twist sts, and pm to mark beg of rnd.
**With A, [knit 1 rnd, purl 1 rnd] twice.
With B, knit 1 rnd, purl 1 rnd.
With A, [knit 1 rnd, purl 1 rnd] twice.**
Begin Triangles Chart Pattern
Beg with rnd 1, work the 8-st rep of chart 18 times. Cont to foll chart in this way, rep rnds 1–8 for a total of 6 reps, then reps rnds 1–4 once more. Change to smaller needle.
Rep from ** to ** for top edge. Bind off knitwise with A.

Finishing
Weave in ends and block piece to knitted measurements. ❖

TRIANGLES CHART

COLOR KEY
☑ A
☐ B

8-st rep

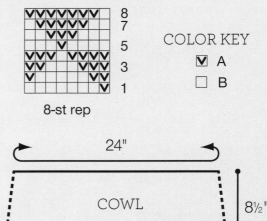

Entrelac Pillows

Entrelac Pillows

Designed by Rosemary Drysdale

Using Noro yarn with an entrelac pattern creates a dazzling display of color and texture that will brighten up any room in your home.

Skill Level

■■■□

Size
Instructions are written for one size.

Knitted Measurements
Approx 17 x 17"/43 x 43cm

Materials
- 4 1¾oz/50g balls (each approx 110yd/100m) of Noro *Silk Garden Lite* (silk, mohair, wool) in #2082 Green/Gold/Blue/Sienna or #2092 Royal/Purple/Green (3)
- One pair size 6 (4mm) needles, OR SIZE TO OBTAIN GAUGE
- 18 x 18"/46 x 46cm pillow form

Gauges
16 sts and 24 rows to 4"/10cm over St st using size 6 (4mm) needles.
2 base triangles to 5"/12.5cm using size 6 (4mm) needles.
TAKE TIME TO CHECK GAUGES.

FRONT
Cast on 56 sts.

Base Triangles
*Row 1 (WS) P2, turn.
Row 2 (RS) K2, turn.
Row 3 P3, turn.
Row 4 K3, turn.
Row 5 P4, turn.
Row 6 K4, turn.
Row 7 P5, turn.
Row 8 K5, turn.
Row 9 P6, turn.
Row 10 K6, turn.
Row 11 P7, turn.
Row 12 K7, turn.
Row 13 P8, do *not* turn.
Rep from * 6 times more—7 triangles made. Turn at end of last row.

**RH Corner Triangle
Row 1 (RS) K2, turn.
Row 2 (WS) P2, turn.
Row 3 Kfb, ssk, turn.
Row 4 P3 turn.
Row 5 Kfb, k1, ssk, turn.
Row 6 P4, turn.
Row 7 Kfb, k2, ssk, turn.
Row 8 P5, turn.
Row 9 Kfb, k3, ssk, turn.
Row 10 P6, turn.
Row 11 Kfb, k4, ssk, turn.
Row 12 P7, turn.
Row 13 Kfb, k5, ssk, do *not* turn.
The RH corner triangle is complete. Leave 8 sts on RH needle.

RS Rectangles
*Pick up row (RS) Pick up and k 8 sts evenly along edge of next triangle/rectangle, turn.
Row 1 (WS) P8, turn.
Row 2 K7, SKP (with last st of rectangle and first st of next triangle), turn.
Rows 3–16 Rep rows 1–2 seven times. Do *not* turn at end of last row.
Rep from * (at pick-up row) 5 times more—6 RH Rectangles made.

LH Corner Triangle
Pick up row (RS) Pick up and k 8 sts along edge of last triangle/rectangle, turn.
Row 1 P2tog, p6, turn.
Row 2 K7, turn.
Row 3 P2tog, p5, turn.
Row 4 K6, turn.

Row 5 P2tog, p4, turn.
Row 6 K5, turn.
Row 7 P2tog, p3, turn.
Row 8 K4, turn.
Row 9 P2tog, p2, turn.
Row 10 K3, turn.
Row 11 P2tog, p1, turn.
Row 12 K2, turn.
Row 13 P2tog, do *not* turn—1 st rem on RH needle.

WS Rectangles

Pick up row (WS) Pick up and p 7 sts evenly along edge of triangle just worked, turn.
*Row 1 (RS) K8, turn.
Row 2 P7, p2tog (with last st of rectangle and first st of next triangle/rectangle), turn.
Rows 3–16 Rep rows 1–2 seven times. Do *not* turn at end of last row.
Next row (WS) Pick up and p 8 sts evenly along edge of next RS rectangle.
Rep from * 6 times more—7 WS rectangles have been made. Turn.
Rep from ** (at RH Corner Triangle) until 7 LH Corner Triangles have been worked and ending with a LH Corner Triangle complete. Do *not* turn and end of last row—1 st rem.

End Triangles

*Pick up row (WS) Pick up and p 7 sts evenly along edge of triangle just worked—8 sts on RH needle. Turn.
Row 1 (RS) K8, turn.
Row 2 P2tog, p5, p2tog, turn.
Row 3 K7, turn.
Row 4 P2tog, p4, p2tog, turn.
Row 5 K6, turn.
Row 6 P2tog, p3, p2tog, turn.
Row 7 K5, turn.
Row 8 P2tog, p2, p2tog, turn.
Row 9 K4, turn.
Row 10 P2tog, p1, p2tog, turn.
Row 11 K3, turn.
Row 12 P2tog, p2tog, turn.
Row 13 K2, turn.
Row 14 P2tog, p2tog, pass 1st st over 2nd st—1 st rem on RH needle.
Rep from * across row, picking up sts along edge of rectangle instead of triangle. Fasten off rem st.

Back

Cast on 72 sts. Work in St st until same length as Front. Bind off sts loosely.

Finishing

Block to knitted measurements. Sew Front and Back tog along 3 sides. Insert pillow form, then sew rem side. ✿

Eyelet Infinity Scarf

Eyelet Infinity Scarf

Designed by Sarah Radow

An eyelet and garter ridge pattern slants diagonally across the fabric, adding texture and visual interest to this wrap-it-twice infinity scarf.

Skill Level
■■□□

Size
Instructions are written for one size.

Knitted Measurements
Circumference 62"/157cm
Width approx 6"/15cm

Materials
- 3 1¾oz/50g balls (each approx 110yd/100m) of Noro *Silk Garden* (silk/mohair/wool) in #373 Blue/Sky Blue/Royal/Light Green (4)
- One pair size 8 (5mm) needles, OR SIZE TO OBTAIN GAUGE
- Tapestry needle

Gauge
14 sts and 24 rows to 4"/10cm over diagonal eyelet pattern stitch using size 8 (5mm) needles. TAKE TIME TO CHECK GAUGE.

Diagonal Eyelet Pattern Stitch
(even number of sts)
Row 1 (RS) K1, M1, k to last 2 sts, k2tog.
Row 2 (WS) Knit.
Row 3 K1, M1, k to last 2 sts, k2tog.
Row 4 Knit.
Row 5 K1, M1, k to last 2 sts, k2tog.
Row 6 *P2tog, yo; rep from * to last 2 sts, end p2.
Row 7 K1, M1, k to last 2 sts, k2tog.
Row 8 Purl.
Rep rows 1–8 for diagonal eyelet pat st.

Note
When the slanted pat st is measured straight across, the actual scarf width measurement is smaller than if it were calculated by the number of sts for the gauge.

Scarf
Cast on 40 sts. Purl 1 row on WS.
Work in diagonal eyelet pat st until piece measures 62"/157cm, measured along one side edge, end with a pat row 8. Do *not* bind off.

Finishing
To finish the scarf, fold the slanted cast-on edge up to match the final row. Then working from the RS, cut yarn, leaving a long end for seaming. Thread end onto tapestry needle then *pull through first st on needle, then insert tapestry needle from front to back to front around the corresponding cast-on st and pull up yarn to join the 2 edges; rep from * until all sts are joined. Weave in ends and block the finished scarf to measurements. ❖

Open Boxy Cardigan

Open Boxy Cardigan

Designed by Mari Lynn Patrick

Garter stitch and stockinette appear in random widths for the body of this cardigan, and the front edges roll neatly back with short-row shaping.

Skill Level
■■■□

Sizes
Instructions are written for size Small (Medium, Large, X-Large, XX-Large, XXX-Large). Shown in size Medium.

Knitted Measurements
Bust (closed) 36 (38, 40, 42, 45, 47½)"/91.5 (96.5, 101.5, 106.5, 114, 120.5)cm
Length 23½ (24, 24½, 25, 26, 26½)"/59.5 (61, 62, 63.5, 66, 67)cm
Upper arm 15 (16, 17, 18, 20, 21)"/38 (40.5, 43, 45.5, 51, 53.5)cm

Materials
- 10 (10, 11, 12, 13, 14) 1¾oz/50g balls (each approx 110yd/100m) Noro *Silk Garden* in #400 Salmon/Magenta/Brown/Yellow (4)
- Two pairs size 8 (5mm) needles, OR SIZE TO OBTAIN GAUGE
- One size 8 (5mm) circular needle, 24"/60cm long
- Stitch holders or waste yarn
- Stitch markers

Gauges
17 sts and 24 rows to 4"/10cm over St st using size 8 (5mm) needles; 17 sts and 30 rows to 4"/10cm over garter st using size 8 (5mm) needles. TAKE TIME TO CHECK GAUGES.

Short Row Wrap & Turn (w & t)
On RS row (on WS row)
1) Wyib (wyif), sl next st purlwise.
2) Move yarn between the needles to the front (back).
3) Sl the same st back to LH needle, turn work. One st is wrapped.
4) When working the wrapped st, insert RH needle under the wrap and work it tog with the corresponding st on needle.

Three-Needle Bind-off
(worked from the RS of work to create a ridge that shows on the RS)
1) Hold WS of pieces tog with needles parallel and the tips facing the same direction. Insert 3rd needle knitwise into the first st on each needle and wrap yarn around needle.
2) Knit the 2 sts tog and sl both off the needles simultaneously. *K the next 2 sts tog in same way.
3) Slip first st on 3rd needle over 2nd st and off the needle, binding off 1 st. Rep from * in step 2 until all sts are bound off.

Body Pattern
Band 1
Beg with a WS row, work 30 rows in garter st.
Band 2
Beg with a WS row, purl 1 row, [knit 1 row, purl 1 row] 15 times, for 31 rows.
Band 3
Work 16 rows in garter st.
Band 4
[Knit 1 row, purl 1 row] 3 times, for 6 rows.
Band 5
Work 16 rows in garter st.
Band 6
[Knit 1 row, purl 1 row] 3 times. Pm each side of last row to mark for armhole, then [knit 1 row, purl 1 row] 3 times, for 12 rows.
Band 7
Work 30 rows in garter st.
Band 8
*Knit 1 row, purl 1 row; rep from * for remainder of piece worked in St st.

Back
Cast on 85 (89, 93, 97, 103, 109) sts. Work in the body pat and, AT SAME TIME, shape the sides as foll: dec 1 st each side on row 2 of

band 2, then rep this dec every 2"/5cm 3 times more—77 (81, 85, 89, 95, 101) sts.

Work even until band 6 is completed. Inc 1 st each side of next row, then rep this inc every 2"/5cm twice more—83 (87, 91, 95, 101, 107) sts. Work even until armhole measures 6½ (7, 7½, 8, 9, 9½)"/16.5 (18, 19, 20.5, 23, 24)cm.

Neck Shaping

Next row (RS) K29 (31, 33, 35, 37, 40), sl center 25 (25, 25, 25, 27, 27) sts to a st holder, join a 2nd ball of yarn and k to end. Working both sides at once, dec 1 st each side every row on the next 5 rows—24 (26, 28, 30, 32, 35) sts rem each side. Leave these sts on hold.

Left Front

Cast on 56 (58, 60, 62, 65, 68) sts.
Row 1 (WS) K26, p1, pm, k29 (31, 33, 35, 38, 41).
Row 2 (RS) K to marker, sl marker, sl 1 wyib, p26. These last 27 sts form the center neck edge worked throughout. Rep rows 1 and 2 for 3 rows more.
Note At this point, while cont to work the pat bands of the body pat as on back, and cont to work the last 27 sts of RS rows in the established pat to end of piece, work short rows to compensate for the garter bands as foll:
*Short row 1 (RS) K to 1 st before the marker, w & t.
Short row 2 K to end. Work 4 rows even, closing up the wrap on the first row.*
Rep from * to * 3 times more.
Note Read before cont to knit.
Then cont in the body pat, dec 1 st at beg of row 2 of band 2 then rep dec every 2"/5cm 3 times more. Then when band 16 is completed, inc 1 st at beg of next RS row, then rep every 2"/5cm twice more and, AT THE SAME TIME, work the same inset of short rows from * to * for 2 reps in band 3 then 2 reps in band 5—52 (54, 56, 58, 61, 64) sts at end of band 5.

Neck Shaping

Neck dec row (RS) Work to 2 sts before the marker, k2tog, sl marker, work to end. Rep the neck dec row every 2"/5cm 3 (3, 3, 3, 4, 4) times more. AT SAME TIME, work the inc at the armhole edge as on back at beg of band 7, then every 2"/5cm twice more AND work 4 sets of (6 row inset) short rows between *'s while working band 7. When same total number of rows are worked as on the back, join the 24 (26, 28, 30, 32, 35) sts of front to back shoulder as foll: From the RS, work 3-needle bind-off joining the shoulders, then sl the sl st over the last bound-off st—27 sts rem. Leave yarn attached. Then to join these 27-st neck edge sts to the back neck, work as foll:

Join Collar to Back Neck

Separately, with circular needle, from the RS and with a separate ball of yarn, pick up and k 6 sts from shaped back neck edge, k25 (25, 25, 25, 27, 27) sts from holder, pick up and k 6 sts from the shaped back neck edge—37 (37, 37, 37, 39, 39) sts.
Return to the 27 sts from left front and work as foll:
Row 1 (RS) Sl 1, p to end.
Row 2 K to the last st, p3tog (working last st tog with 2 sts on circular needle from the back neck), turn.
Row 3 Sl 1, p to end.
Row 4 K to last st, then p2tog (working last st tog with 1 st on circular needle from the back neck), turn. Rep rows 1–4 until all back neck sts are worked. Leave the 27 sts on hold along with the right shoulder sts.

Right Front

Cast on 56 (58, 60, 62, 65, 68) sts.
Row 1 (WS) K29 (31, 33, 35, 38, 41), pm, p1, k26.
Row 2 (RS) P26, sl 1 wyib, pm, k to end.
Cont as for left front, reversing all shaping and with the short rows along the garter bands being worked first on the WS row, then the RS row. When right front measures same as back, use the 3-needle bind-off from the RS to join the 24 (26, 28, 30, 32, 35) shoulder sts and the 27 sts from the neck trim.

Sleeves

Cast on 55 (59, 63, 67, 75, 79) sts.
Band 1
Beg with a WS row, work 15 rows in garter st.
Band 2
Inc row (RS) K1, kfb, k to last 2 sts, kfb, k1. Cont in St st, rep inc row every 12th row once more.
Band 3
Work 15 rows in garter st, rep inc row on the last row. Work 14 rows in garter st.
Band 4
Rep inc row on next row. Then cont in St st, rep inc row every 12th row once more—65 (69, 73, 77, 85, 89) sts.
When sleeve measures 12"/30.5cm from beg, lay piece aside. Then, to join sleeves to armhole, from the RS with circular needle, pick up and k 65 (69, 73, 77, 85, 89) sts between the markers from armhole edge. Then from the RS, join the top of sleeve to the armhole using 3-needle bind-off. Work other sleeve in same way.

Finishing

Weave in ends. Lightly steam block the cardigan from the WS, taking care not to press the front rolled edges. Sew side and sleeve seams. ❖

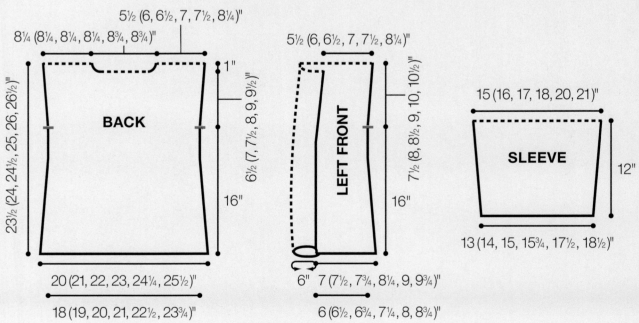

BACK

5½ (6, 6½, 7, 7½, 8¼)"

8¼ (8¼, 8¼, 8¼, 8¾, 8¾)"

1"

6½ (7, 7½, 8, 9, 9½)"

23½ (24, 24½, 25, 26, 26½)"

16"

20 (21, 22, 23, 24¼, 25½)"

18 (19, 20, 21, 22½, 23¾)"

LEFT FRONT

5½ (6, 6½, 7, 7½, 8¼)"

7½ (8, 8½, 9, 10, 10½)"

16"

6" 7 (7½, 7¾, 8¼, 9, 9¾)"

6 (6½, 6¾, 7¼, 8, 8¾)"

SLEEVE

15 (16, 17, 18, 20, 21)"

12"

13 (14, 15, 15¾, 17½, 18½)"

89

Fingerless Gloves

Stitch Glossary

2-st RPC Sl 1 st to cn and hold to *back*, k1, p1 from cn.
2-st LPC Sl 1 st to cn and hold to *front*, p1, k1 from cn.
8-st RC Sl 4 sts to cn and hold to *back*, k4, k4 from cn.
8-st LC Sl 4 sts to cn and hold to *front*, k4, k4 from cn.
M1 p-st (make 1 purl stitch) Insert LH needle from back to front under the horizontal bar between the last st worked and the next st on LH needle, p1 through the front loop to M1 p-st.
M1R (make 1 right) Insert LH needle from back to front under the horizontal bar between the last st worked and the next st on LH needle, k1 through the front loop to M1R.
M1L (make 1 left) Insert LH needle from front to back under the horizontal bar between the last st worked and the next st on LH needle, k1 through back loop to M1L.

Gauge

20 sts and 34 rnds to 4"/10cm over pat sts foll charts, using size 4 (3.5mm) needles. TAKE TIME TO CHECK GAUGE.

Lace Trim

Rnd 1 Purl.
Rnd 2 *K2tog, yo; rep from * around.
Bind off all sts purlwise.

Left Glove

With dpn, beg at the cuff edge, cast on 40 sts. Divide sts onto 3 dpn with 15 sts on Needle 1 for palm side, 12 sts on Needle 2 for right side of the glove front, and 13 sts on Needle 3 for left side of the glove front. Join to work in rnds, taking care not to twist sts on needles, and pm to mark beg of rnd.
Begin Chart 1
Rnd 1 *Needle 1* K1, [p1, k1] 7 times; *Needle 2* K1, k2tog, yo, p2, k2, p2, k1tbl, p1, k1tbl; *Needle 3* [P1, k1tbl] twice, p2, k2, p2, SKP, yo, k1. Needles 2 and 3 are the first rnd of chart 1 for the glove front. Cont to foll chart 1 in this way, rep rnds 1–4 for the glove front and cont in k1, p1 rib for the palm side, until piece measures 6"/15cm from beg.
Begin Chart 2
Rnd 1 *Needle 1* K15; *Needle 2* K1, k2tog, yo, p1, M1 p-st, k8; *Needle 3* P1, k8, M1 p-st, p1, k2tog, yo, k1—13 sts on Needle 2 and 14 sts on Needle 3 for working chart 2.
Cont to work chart 2 pat in this way (with 15 sts for palm in St st) until all 11 rnds of chart 2 are complete.
Note Cont to work the 15 palm sts on Needle 1 in St st (k every rnd), while working the charts for the rem of the glove front.
Begin chart 3
Rnds 1–15 Working the 15 sts on Needle 1 in St st, work Needles 2 and 3 in the 27-st chart 3 pat for these rnds.

Fingerless Gloves

Designed by Jacqueline van Dillen

Fit for the dramatic gesture, cables mingle with wavy eyelets and twisted ribs to define the fronts of these ¾-length fingerless gloves.

Skill Level
■■■□

Size
Instructions are written for one size.

Knitted Measurements
Circumference 7½"/19cm
Total Length 11¾"/30cm

Materials
■ 1 3½oz/100g ball (each approx 328yd/300m) of Noro *Silk Garden Sock* (wool/silk/polyamide/mohair) in #354 Purple/Green/Blue **(2)**
■ One set (4) size 4 (3.5mm) double-pointed needles (dpn), OR SIZE TO OBTAIN GAUGE
■ Waste yarn
■ Stitch markers
■ Cable needle (cn)
■ 1 Spool of black elastic thread

Begin Thumb Chart

Note Thumb chart is worked simultaneously with chart 3, inserted into the chart opening beg on rnd 6.

Rnd 6 *Needle 1* K15; *Needle 2* K1, then foll rnd 6 of thumb chart as foll: M1R, k2, yo, M1L; then, beg with st 4 of chart 3 rnd 6, work through st 13; *Needle 3* Work sts 14–27 of chart 3 rnd 6.

Rnd 7 *Needle 1* K15; *Needle 2* K1, then k5 foll thumb chart, work rnd 7 of chart 3 through st 13; *Needle 3* Work sts 14–27 of chart 3 rnd 7.

Rnds 8–16 Cont to foll chart 3 and the inset thumb chart sts as established—15 thumb sts at the end of rnd 16. At the end of rnd 16, transfer the 15 sts for thumb to waste yarn for completing later.

Begin Chart 4

Rnd 1 *Needle 1* K15; *Needle 2* K1, cast on 2 sts to close up the thumb opening, p2, k8; *Needle 3* P1, k8, p2, k3—42 sts. Cont to work chart 4, working rnds 2–11 of the chart on the glove front and cont to work the 15 palm sts in St st.

Begin Chart 5

Next 8 rnds Work the first 15 sts on Needle 1 in St st and the 27 sts on Needles 2 and 3 in chart 5 pat for 2 (4-rnd) reps. Then, work the lace trim for 2 rnds and bind off purlwise.

Thumb—Begin Chart 6

Sl the 15 thumb sts onto 2 dpn and pick up and k 2 more sts at base of thumb—17 sts. Divide the sts evenly onto 3 dpn. Join to work in rnds and work foll chart 6 for 10 rnds. Then work lace trim for 2 rnds and bind off purlwise.

Right Glove

Beg at the cuff edge, cast on 40 sts onto 3 dpn with 12 sts on Needle 1 for right side of the glove front, 13 sts on Needle 2 for left side of the glove front, and 15 sts on Needle 3 for the palm side. Cont to work as for left glove, with sts for charts and the palm side repositioned in this way, through completion of chart 2.

Begin Chart 3

Rnds 1–5 Work the sts on Needles 1 and 2 over 27 sts of chart 3 and the sts on Needle 3 in St st for these rows.

Begin Thumb Chart

Thumb chart is worked simultaneously with chart 3, and inserted into the chart opening on sts 25 and 26 (instead of sts 2 and 3) for opposite-side placement of the thumb, and working the 2-st eyelet over sts 2 and 3 of chart 3 (instead of sts 25 and 26). Cont to work as for the left glove with reversed placement of thumb.

Finishing

Weave in ends and block finished pieces to knitted measurements. To give elasticity to the edge, weave a strand of elastic thread along the top of the hand opening. ❧

CHART 1

25 sts

CHART 2

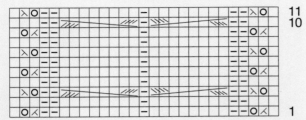

27 sts

CHART 6

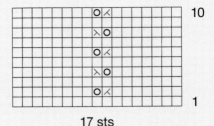

17 sts

CHART 3 - Left Glove

Right glove ↓

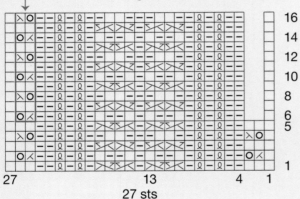

27   13   4   1

27 sts

THUMBS CHART

15 sts

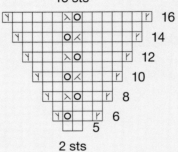

2 sts

CHART 4

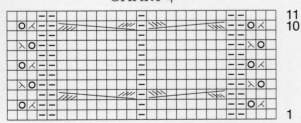

27 sts

STITCH KEY

- ☐ knit
- − purl
- ☉ yo
- ⊠ k2tog
- ⊠ ssk
- ⊠ SKP
- ℧ k1 tbl
- Ƴ M1R
- ⅄ M1L
- ⊠⊠ 2-st RPC
- ⊠⊠ 2-st LPC
- ⊠⊠⊠ 8-st RC
- ⊠⊠⊠ 8-st LC

CHART 5

27 sts

Gothic Shawl

Gothic Shawl

Designed by Terri Rosenthal

Multiple knitting and stitch techniques are splendidly on display throughout this shawl that wraps the body and fastens with two buttons at the front.

Skill Level
■■■■

Size
Instructions are written for one size.

Knitted Measurements
Length (at top edge) 70"/178cm
Depth (at center) 30"/76cm

Materials
- 6 1¾oz/50g balls (each approx 110yd/100m) of Noro *Silk Garden* (wool/mohair/silk) in #2088 Navy/Aquas/Browns/Greys (4)
- One size 8 (5mm) circular needle, 40"/100cm long, OR SIZE TO OBTAIN GAUGE
- Stitch markers
- Two 1¼"/32mm buttons

Stitch Glossary
M4R (M5R, M6R) [Insert LH needle from front to back under horizontal bar between last st worked and next st on LH needle, k1tbl, let horizontal bar slip off LH needle] 4 (5, 6) times for M4R (M5R, M6R). This creates a round eyelet hole and increases 4 (5, 6) sts. **Note** Always pick up the same horizontal bar for each k1tbl.
MB (make bobble) K1 into front, back, front, and back of the same st (to make 4 sts from 1 st), turn, p4; turn, k4; turn, p4; turn, k4tog—1 st rem.
Sl st over Using the last 2 sts on RH needle, lift the first st on RH needle over the last st worked to dec 1 more st; or when working the bobble, use this sl st dec method to dec the next K1 st after the bobble.

Gauge
14 sts and 26 rows to 4"/10cm over garter st, after blocking, using size 8 (5mm) needle. TAKE TIME TO CHECK GAUGE.

Note
Begin shawl at the lower ruffle edge and work the diminished ruffle edge first, then the ridge pat to complete this edge. Stitches are then worked in garter st, using short rows from the center outwards to each side edge (see schematic), until all sts are worked to the ends. Then, using the extra length of yarn left over from the cast-on edge to pick up along the top of the right hand edge, the top edge sts are worked for the top lace pattern trim. Read entire pat before beg.

Shawl
Beg at the outer edge, using the long-tail cast-on method, measure approx 200"/508cm of yarn and cast on 400 sts. There should be at least 12"/30.5cm extra length leftover at the end (for the top edge pick-up described in the note above).
Row 1 (RS) P6, [k2, p4, k2, p10] 10 times; k2, p4, k2, p12; [k2, p4, k2, p10] 10 times, end k2, p4, k2, p6.
Row 2 K6, [p2, k4, p2, k10] 10 times; p2, k4, p2, k12; [p2, k4, p2, k10] 10 times, end p2, k4, p2, k6.
Row 3 P6, [k2, p2, M6R, p2, k2, p3tog, bind off 3 purlwise, p3tog, sl st over] 10 times; k2, p2, M6R, p2, k2, p4tog, bind off 3 sts purlwise, p4tog, sl st over; [k2, p2, M6R, p2, k2, p3tog, bind off 3 sts purlwise, p3tog, sl st over] 10 times, end k2, p2, M6R, p2, k2, p6.
Row 4 K6, [p2, k10, p2, k1, cast on 2 sts, k1] 21 times, end p2, k10, p2, k6—404 sts.
Row 5 P6, [k2, p10, k2, p4] 21 times, end k2, p10, k2, p6.
Row 6 K6, [p2, k10, p2, k4] 21 times, end p2, k10, p2, k6.
Row 7 Rep row 5.
Row 8 K6, [p2, k10, p2, k4] 10 times, p2, k10, p2, k1, k2tog, k1, [p2,

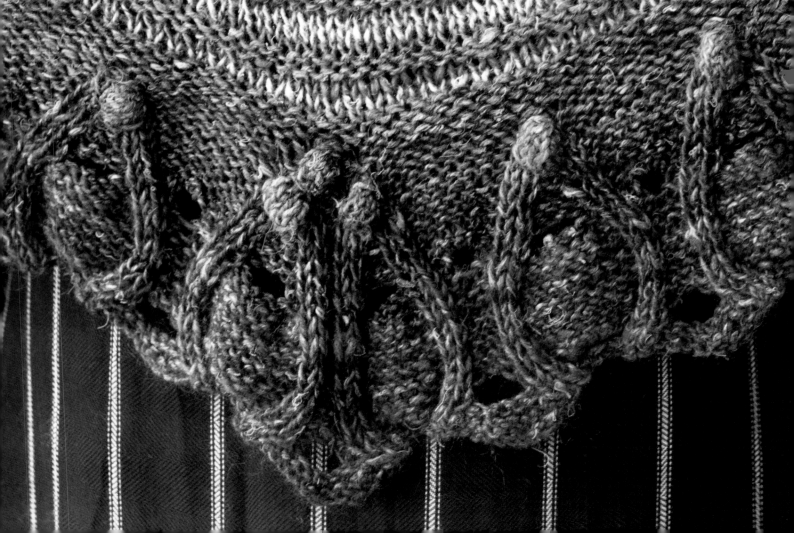

k10, p2, k4] 10 times, end p2, k10, p2, k6—403 sts.

Row 9 P6, [k2, p10, k2, p4] 10 times, k2, p10, k2, p3, [k2, p10, k2, p4] 10 times, end k2, p10, k2, p6.

Row 10 K6, [p2, k10, p2, k4] 10 times, p2, k10, p2, k3, [p2, k10, p2, k4] 10 times, end p2, k10, p2, k6.

Row 11 Rep row 9.

Row 12 Rep row 10.

Row 13 P6, [k2, p3tog, bind off 3 sts purlwise, p3tog, sl st over, k2, p2, M4R, p2] 10 times, k2, p3tog, bind off 3 sts purlwise, p3tog, sl st over, k2, p1, p2tog, [k2, p3tog, bind off 3 sts purlwise, p3tog, sl st over, k2, p2, M4R, p2] 10 times, end k2, p3tog, bind off 3 sts purlwise, p3tog, sl st over, k2, p6.

Row 14 K6, [p2, k1, cast on 2 sts, k1, p2, k8] 10 times, p2, k1, cast on 2 sts, k1, p2, k2, [p2, k1, cast on 2 sts, k1, p2, k8] 10 times, end p2, k1, cast on 2 sts, k1, p2, k6—350 sts.

Row 15 P6, [k2, p4, k2, p8] 10 times, k2, p4, k2, p2, [k2, p4, k2, p8] 10 times, end k2, p4, k2, p6.

Row 16 K6, [p2, k4, p2, k8] 10 times, p2, k4, p2, k2, [p2, k4, p2, k8] 10 times, end p2, k4, p2, k6.

Row 17 P6, [k2, (p2tog) twice, k2, p8] 10 times, k2, (p2tog) twice, k2, p2, [k2, (p2tog) twice, k2, p8] 10 times, end k2 (p2tog) twice, k2, p6—306 sts.

Row 18 K6, [p2, k2tog, p2, k8] 10 times, p2, k2tog, p2, k2, [p2, k2tog, p2, k8] 10 times, end p2, k2tog, p2, k6—284 sts.

Row 19 P6, [k2, k2tog, k1, p8] 10 times, k2, k2tog, k1, p2, [k2, k2tog, k1, p8] 10 times, end k2, k2tog, k1, p6—262 sts.

Row 20 K6, [(p2tog) twice, k8] 10 times, (p2tog) twice k2, [(p2tog) twice, k8] 10 times, end (p2tog) twice, k6—218 sts.

Bobble row 21 P6, [MB, k1, sl st over, p8] 10 times, MB, k1, sl st over, p2, [MB, k1, sl st over, p8] 10 times, end MB, k1, sl st over, p6—196 sts.

Row 22 (WS) K98, pm (to mark the center), k2tog, k96—195 sts.

Bobble row 23 (RS) P to 2 sts before the center marker, p2tog, sl marker, MB, k1, sl st over, p2tog, p to end—192 sts, with 96 sts each side of the center marker.

Row 24 Knit.

Row 25 Purl.

Begin Ridge Pattern

Row 26 (WS) Purl.

Row 27 (RS) Knit.

Row 28 Purl.

Row 29 Purl.

Row 30 Knit.

Row 31 Knit.

Row 32 Purl.

Row 33 Knit.

Row 34 Knit.

Row 35 Purl.

Row 36 Knit.

Begin Central Short-Row Pattern

Note At the end of every short row, turn, but do not wrap the st. Using this method, the sts from the border will be worked into and added incrementally as described. Use markers to keep track, if necessary.

Short row 37 (RS) P to 3 sts before center marker, k3, sl marker, k3, turn.

Short row 38 (WS) K12, turn.

Short row 39 K18, turn.

Short row 40 K21, turn.

Short row 41 K24, turn.

Short row 42 K27, turn.

Short row 43 K30, turn.

Short row 44 K32, turn.

Short row 45 K34, turn.

Short row 46 K36, turn.

Short row 47 K38, turn.

Short row 48 K40, turn.

Short row 49 K42, turn.

Short row 50 K44, turn.

Short row 51 K46, turn.

Short rows 52–69 Cont to k 2 more sts from the edge on each of these 18 short rows, having 82 on the last short row 69.

Short rows 70–180 K 1 more st from the edge on each of these 110 short rows, with all 192 sts incorporated on the last WS row.

Row 181 (RS) Using the end from the cast-on edge, pick up and k 29 sts along the side edge of the lower ruffle, k192 sts, then pick up and k 29 sts from the side edge of the lower ruffle—250 sts.

Row 182 (WS) Knit.

Begin Top Edge Border

Row 183 K4, *k2, M5R, k6; rep from *, end k2, M5R, k4.

Row 184 Purl.

Row 185 Knit.

Bind off all sts loosely.

Finishing

Weave in ends and block shawl to measurements, pinning out each ruffle point until dry. Sew buttons for front closure as pictured. ❖

SHAWL

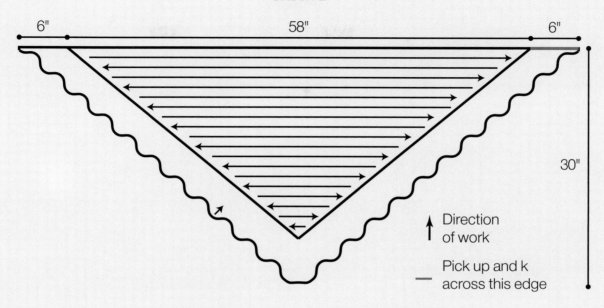

6" 58" 6"

30"

↑ Direction
of work

— Pick up and k
across this edge

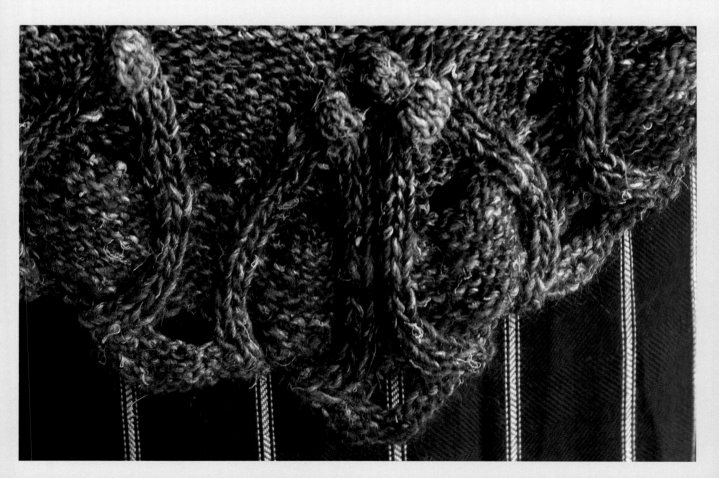

Sunburst Shawl

Sunburst Shawl

Designed by Jacqueline van Dillen

Indulge your flair for the dramatic with this sweeping sunburst shawl, knit seamlessly with panels of short-row shaping worked on the bias.

Skill Level
■■■□

Size
Instructions are written for one size.

Knitted Measurements
Length (measured while laid flat) 53"/135cm
Depth 23½"/60cm

Materials
■ 2 3½oz/100g balls (each approx 328yd/300m) of Noro *Silk Garden Sock* (wool/silk/polyamide/mohair) in #415 Peach/Pink/Purple (2)
■ One size 6 (4mm) circular needle, 24"/60cm long, OR SIZE TO OBTAIN GAUGE
■ One size ¾"/2cm pom-pom maker

Gauge
20 sts and 34 rows to 4"/10cm over garter st using size 6 (4mm) needle. TAKE TIME TO CHECK GAUGE.

Note
Add one additional ball of yarn to make a shawl with more drape (approx 26½"/68cm additional length). See Diagram.

Short Row Wrap & Turn (w & t)
On RS row (on WS row)
1) Wyib (wyif), sl next st purlwise.
2) Move yarn between the needles to the front (back).
3) Sl the same st back to LH needle, turn work–one st is wrapped.
4) When working the wrapped st, insert RH needle under the wrap and work it tog with the corresponding st on needle.

Sloped Bind-off
1) One row *before* the bind-off row, work to the last st of the row. Do *not* work this st. Turn work.
2) Wyib, sl first st from left needle knitwise.
3) Pass unworked st of previous row over the slipped st–1 st is bound off. Cont to bind off desired number of sts in the normal way.

Shawl
Cast on 120 sts.
Rows 1 and 2 Knit.
**Short row 3 K110, w & t.
Short row 4 K to end of row.
Short row 5 K100, w & t.
Short row 6 and all even (WS) rows K to end of row.
Short row 7 K90, w & t.
Short row 9 K80, w & t.
Short row 11 K70, w & t.
Short row 13 K60, w & t.
Short row 15 K50, w & t.
Short row 17 K40, w & t.
Short row 19 K30, w & t.
Short row 21 K20, w & t.
Short row 23 K10, w & t.
Row 25 (RS) K to end of entire row on all 120 sts, closing up the wraps.
Row 26 (WS) Bind off 3 sts using sloped bind-off method, k to end of row.

Row 27 (RS) Cast on 5 sts, k to end of row.
Row 28 (WS) Bind off 2 sts using sloped bind-off method, k to end of entire row—120 sts.**

Rep from ** to ** until there are a total of 14 stepped short-row wedges, ending with row 25 of the 15th short row wedge (or, for the longer version, a total of 22 stepped short-row wedges).

Finish the 15th Short-Row Wedge
Row 26 (WS) Bind off 12 sts using the sloped bind-off method, k to end of row.
Row 27 (RS) Knit.
Row 28 (WS) Bind off 12 sts using sloped bind-off method, k to end of row—96 sts.

Begin the 16th Short-Row Wedge
Short row 3 K88, w & t.
Short row 4 and all even (WS) short rows K to end of row.
Short row 5 K80, w & t.
Short row 7 K72, w & t.
Short row 9 K64, w & t.
Short row 11 K56, w & t.
Short row 13 K48, w & t.
Short row 15 K40, w & t.
Short row 17 K32, w & t.
Short row 19 K24, w & t.
Short row 21 K16, w & t.
Short row 23 K8, w & t.
Row 25 (RS) K to end of entire row on all 96 sts, closing up the wraps.
Row 26 (WS) Bind off 12 sts using sloped bind-off method, k to end of row.
Row 27 (RS) Knit.
Row 28 (WS) Bind off 12 sts using sloped bind-off method, k to end of row—72 sts.

Begin the 17th Short-Row Wedge
Short row 3 K66, w & t.
Short row 4 and all even (WS) short rows K to end of row.
Short row 5 K60, w & t.
Short row 7 K54, w & t.
Short row 9 K48, w & t.
Short row 11 K42, w & t.
Short row 13 K36, w & t.

Short row 15 K30, w & t.
Short row 17 K24, w & t.
Short row 19 K18, w & t.
Short row 21 K12, w & t.
Short row 23 K6, w & t.
Row 25 K to end of row, closing up the wraps. Bind off all 72 sts.

Finishing
Weave in ends and block finished piece to measurements. Make 3 small pompoms, using the green section of the yarn. Attach one pompon to each of the 3 points of the shawl. ✤

DIAGRAM

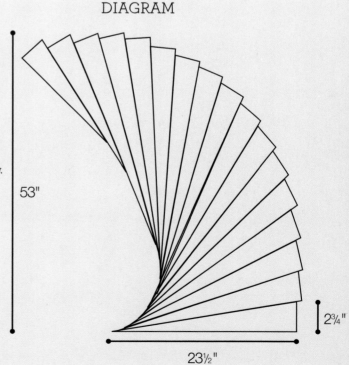

53"

2¾"

23½"

Smock Stitch Cowl

Smock Stitch Cowl

Designed by Anna Davis

Textured smock stitch is framed by garter-stitch bands that add a slight flare to the top and bottom of this cozy cowl.

Skill Level
■■□□

Size
Instructions are written for one size.

Knitted Measurements
Circumference (outer edges) 39"/99cm
Circumference (center) 36"/91.5cm
Height 10¾"/27cm

Materials
■ 4 1¾oz/50g balls (each approx 137yd/125cm) of Noro *Silk Garden Lite* (silk/mohair/wool) in #2086 Orange/Purple/Tan
■ One size 8 (5mm) circular needle, 32"/80cm long, OR SIZE TO OBTAIN GAUGE
■ Stitch marker

Gauge
21 sts and 26 rnds to 4"/10cm over smock stitch pat, after blocking, using size 8 (5mm) needles. TAKE TIME TO CHECK GAUGE.

Cable Cast-on
Place slip knot on LH needle, k1 and pull up a loop but do not remove st from LH needle, place this loop on LH needle. There are now 2 sts on LH needle. *Insert RH needle between the 2 sts and wrap yarn and needle and pull up a st between these 2 sts, transfer the st to LH needle for 1 cast-on st; rep from * until required number of sts are cast on.

Elastic Bind-off
K1, *k1 and pull up a loop but do not remove st from LH needle; then with LH needle sl the first worked st on RH needle over the 2nd st on RH needles—1 st is bound off and 1 st rem on RH needle. Pull the st off LH needle; rep from * around until all sts are bound off *and* work the final bound-off st into the first bound-off st to avoid a "jog." Pull yarn through final st and fasten off.

Garter Stitch
(worked in rnds)
Rnd 1 Knit.
Rnd 2 Purl.
Rep these 2 rnds for garter st worked in rnds.

Smocking Stitch
Wyib, insert RH needle from front to back in between the 6th and 7th sts on LH needle, wrap yarn around needle as if to knit and pull up a long loop between these 2 sts. Place loop at the tip of LH needle (being sure that loop is not too tight), then k this loop tog with next st on LH needle, then k1, p2, k2.

Smock Stitch Pattern
(multiple of 8 sts)
Rnd 1 *P2, k2; rep from * around.
Rnds 2 and 3 Rep rnd 1.

Smock rnd 4 *P2, work smocking st over the next 6 sts; rep from * around.

Rnds 5 and 6 Rep rnd 1.

Rnd 7 *P2, k2; rep from * to the last 2 sts, then place new marker so that the last 2 sts are repositioned to become the first 2 sts of rnd 8. (The beg-of-rnd marker on rnd 8 will stay in place, as the marker is only repositioned on this rnd.)

Smock rnd 8 *Work smocking st over 6 sts, p2; rep from * to the last 2 sts, end k2 (this is with the repositioning of the beg-of-rnd marker). Rep rnds 1–8 for smock stitch pattern.

Cowl

Using the cable cast-on method, cast on 192 sts. Join to work in rnds, taking care not to twist sts on needle, and pm to mark beg of rnd. Work 9 rnds in garter st.

Begin Smock Stitch Pattern

Work in smock stitch pat, rep the 8-rnd pat for 6 reps. Then, work rnds 1–6 once more. Then, work 9 rnds in garter st. Bind off using the elastic bind-off method.

Finishing

Weave in ends and block the finished cowl to measurements. ✤

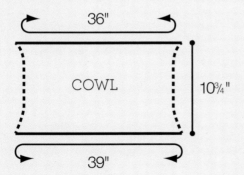

36"

COWL

10¾"

39"

Brioche Rib Hat

Brioche Rib Hat

Designed by Therese Chynoweth

Stay warm in this brioche rib hat that's guaranteed to provide deep cover for all of your good and bad hair days.

Skill Level
■■■■

Size
Instructions are written for one size.

Knitted Measurements
Circumference 22"/56cm
Depth 10"/25.5cm

Materials
- 1 3½oz/100g ball (each approx 328yd/300m) of Noro *Silk Garden Sock* (wool/silk/polyamide/mohair) in #407 Brown/Purple/White/Green (A) ②
- 1 3½ oz/100g ball (each approx 328yd/300m) of Noro *Silk Garden Sock Solo* (wool/silk/polyamide/mohair) in #10 Pink (B) ②
- One each sizes 3 and 6 (3.25 and 4mm) circular needle, each 16"/40cm long, OR SIZE TO OBTAIN GAUGE
- One set (5) size 3 (2.5mm) double-pointed needles (dpn)
- Stitch marker

Stitch Glossary
Brk1 (brioche knit 1) Knit the next st tog with the yo.
Brp1 (brioche purl 1) Purl the next st tog with the yo.
Sl 1 yo (slip 1, yo) Sl 1 st purlwise and bring yarn over needle from front to back (if the next st is a knit st) or around and under needle to front (if the next st is a purl st).
Brl sl dec (brioche left slanting 2-st dec) Slip next brk st knitwise, brk the next 2 sts tog, pass the slipped brk st over—2 sts dec'd.
Br k2tog (brioche k2tog) K the next st and the brk st tog—1 st dec'd.

Gauge
20 sts and 52 rnds to 4"/10cm over brioche rib pat using size 3 (3.25mm) needles. TAKE TIME TO CHECK GAUGE.

Two-color Brioche Rib Pattern Stitch
(multiple of 2 sts)
Rnd 1 With A, *brk1, yarn forward, sl 1 yo; rep from * around.
Rnd 2 With B, *yarn forward, sl 1 yo, b1p1; rep from * around.
Rep rnds 1 and 2 for two-color brioche rib pat st. **Note** These 2 rnds will count as 1 rnd on the RS if you are counting the knit "V" sts to determine row gauge.

Note
The 52 rnds that constitute the 4"/10cm row gauge will actually count as 26 rnds on the RS.

Hat
Using larger circular needle, work the 2-color cast-on using the long-tail cast-on method as foll: make a slip knot with A and place on needle, then make a slip knot with B and place on needle, *separate the 2 strands of B and bring the 2 strands of A between B, hold strands as for a long-tail cast-on and cast on 1 st with A, separate the 2 strands of A and bring the 2 strands of B between A, hold strands as for a long-tail cast-on and cast on 1 st with B; rep from * 53 times more—110 sts. Join, taking care not to twist sts, and pm to mark beg of rnd. Change to smaller circular needle.
Set-up rnd 1 With A, *k1, yarn forward, sl 1 yo; rep from * around.
Set-up rnd 2 With B, *yarn forward, sl 1 yo, brp1; rep from * around.
Work in two-color brioche rib pat st, rep rnds 1 and 2 until piece measures 7¾"/19.5cm from beg, end with rnd 2 in B.

Top Shaping

Note Change to dpn when there are too few sts to fit comfortably on the circular needle.

Dec rnd 1 With A, *brl sl dec, work next 9 sts, brl sl dec, work next 7 sts; rep from * around—90 sts.

Next rnd With B, rep pat rnd 2. Then work 3 more reps of the 2-row pat rep.

Dec rnd 2 With A, *work next 7 sts, brl sl dec, work next 5 sts, brl sl dec; rep from * to the last 17 sts, then work next 7 sts, brl sl dec, work next 5 sts, sl 2 knitwise and remove beg of rnd marker, sl the 2nd st back to LH needle and brk the next 2 sts tog, psso and pm for new beg of rnd—70 sts.

Next rnd With B, *yarn forward, brp1, sl 1 yo; rep from * around. Then, work 2 more reps of the 2-rnd pat rep.

Dec rnd 3 With A, br k2tog, *work next 5 sts, brl sl dec, work next 3 sts, brl sl dec; rep from * to the last 15 sts, work next 5 sts, brl sl dec, work next 3 sts, sl 1, remove beg of rnd marker, sl 1, pass first st over 2nd st, sl this st back to LH needle, pm for new beg of rnd—50 sts.

Next rnd With B, *yarn forward, sl 1 yo, brp1; rep from * around. Then, work 2 more reps of the 2-rnd pat rep.

Dec rnd 4 With A, remove beg of rnd marker, sl 1, place new beg of rnd marker, *work next 3 sts, brl sl dec, work next st, brl sl dec; rep from * 4 times more—30 sts.

Next rnd With B, *yarn forward, brp1, sl 1 yo; rep from * around. Then, work 1 more rep of the 2-rnd pat rep.

Dec rnd 5 With A, *work 3 sts, brl sl dec; rep from * around—20 sts.

Next rnd With B, *yarn forward, brp1, sl 1 yo; rep from * around.

Dec rnd 6 With A, [k2tog] 5 times—10 sts. Pull through sts on needles once then pull through sts again and draw up tightly to close top.

Finishing

Weave in ends and block hat to knitted measurements. ✤

Embroidered Mittens

Embroidered Mittens

Designed by Lidia Karabinech

Add a touch of whimsy to a basic mitten design, with pretty bouquets of embroidered wildflowers tied up with chain-stitch bows.

Skill Level
■■□□

Sizes
Instructions are written for Woman's size Small (Medium, Large). Shown in size Small.

Knitted Measurements
Circumference 6½ (7¼, 8)"/16.5 (18.5, 20.5) cm
Total Length 9¼ (9½, 9¾)"/23.5 (24, 25) cm

Materials
- 1 3½oz/100g ball (each approx 328yd/300m) of Noro *Silk Garden Sock Solo* (wool/silk/polyamide/mohair) in #6 Dark Brown (A) 🧶2
- 1 3½oz/100g ball (each approx 328yd/300m) of Noro *Silk Garden Sock* (wool/silk/polyamide/mohair) in #411 Purples/Green/Grey (B) 🧶2
- One set (5) size 4 (3.5mm) double-pointed needles (dpn), OR SIZE TO OBTAIN GAUGE
- One size B/1 (2mm) crochet hook
- Stitch markers
- Waste yarn
- Tapestry needle

Stitch Glossary
M1R (make 1 right) Insert LH needle from back to front under the horizontal bar between the last st worked and the next st on LH needle, k1 through the front loop to M1R.
M1L (make 1 left) Insert LH needle from front to back under the horizontal bar between the last st worked and the next st on LH needle, k1 through back loop to M1L.

Gauge
20 sts and 30 rnds to 4"/10cm over St st using size 4 (3.5mm) needles. TAKE TIME TO CHECK GAUGE.

Right Mitten
With A, cast on 32 (36, 40) sts evenly onto 4 dpn with 8 (9, 10) sts on each needle. Join to work in rnds, taking care not to twist sts, and pm to mark beg of rnd.
Rnd 1 *K1, p1; rep from * around. Cont in k1, p1 rib until piece measures 2½"/6.5cm from beg. Remainder of mitten is worked in St st (k every rnd).

Thumb Gusset
Set-up rnd 1 K2, pm for gusset, k2, pm for gusset, k to end of needle 2, then pm for side marker, k to end of rnd.
Rnd 2 K2, sl marker, M1R, k to 2nd marker, M1L, sl marker, k to end of rnd.
Rnds 3–5 Knit.
Rep rnds 2–5 until there are 10 sts between the 2 gusset markers and a total of 40 (44, 48) sts. Work even until piece measures 2½"/6.5cm above the ribbed cuff.
Next rnd K to the first gusset marker, remove marker, M1R, transfer the next 10 sts (up to the next marker) to waste yarn for thumb, cast on 2 sts, remove 2nd marker, M1L, k to end of rnd—34 (38, 42) sts. Work even until piece measures 6"/15cm above the cuff.

Top Shaping
Dec rnd 1 [Ssk, k13 (15, 17), k2tog] twice—30 (34, 38) sts.
Rnd 2 and every even rnd Knit.
Dec rnd 3 [Ssk, k11 (13, 15), k2tog] twice—26 (30, 34) sts.
Dec rnd 5 [Ssk, k9 (11, 13), k2tog] twice—22 (26, 30) sts.
Next 3 (4, 5) odd numbered rnds Dec as previous dec rnd, with 2 fewer sts between each set of dec's on each of the 3 (4, 5) dec rnds—10 sts rem. Cut yarn leaving a long end. Join top of mitten using Kitchener stitch (*see page 36*).

Thumb
Transfer the 10 sts from waste yarn to 2 dpn (5 sts on each dpn), then pick up and k 3 sts at base of thumb on 3rd dpn—13 sts. Join and pm to mark beg of rnd. Work even in St st (k every rnd) for 2½"/6.5cm.
Dec rnd [K3, k2tog] twice, k3—11 sts.

Next rnd Knit.

Dec rnd [K1, k2tog] 3 times, k2—8 sts.
Cut yarn, leaving a long end. Join top of thumb using Kitchener stitch.

Left Mitten

Work same as right mitten to the thumb gusset.

Thumb Gusset

Set-up rnd 1 K to 4 sts before end of rnd, pm for gusset, k2, pm for gusset, k2.

Rnd 2 K to first gusset marker, sl marker, M1R, k to 2nd gusset marker, M1L, sl marker, k to end of rnd.

Rnds 3–5 Knit.

Rep rnds 2–5 until there are 10 sts between the 2 gusset markers and a total of 40 (44, 48) sts. Work even until piece measures 2½"/6.5cm from the end of the cuff.

Next rnd K to the first gusset marker, remove marker, M1R, transfer the next 10 sts (up to the next marker) to waste yarn for thumb, cast on 2 sts, remove 2nd marker, M1L, k to end of rnd—34 (38, 42) sts. Complete hand, top shaping, and thumb as for right mitten.

Finishing

Weave in ends and block pieces to measurements. Embroider the mittens foll the diagram and photo as a guide (select colors from the color B as in photo). When working the straight st for all three flowers, *work the first half of the petal on the RS, slide tapestry needle under 1 st; work the 2nd half of the petal on the RS*; rep from * to * until all 8 petals are complete. For the chain ties (make 2), with crochet hook, make a 12"/30.5cm chain. Pull through the base of the bouquet and tie in a bow at front. Knot each end of the chain to secure. ❖

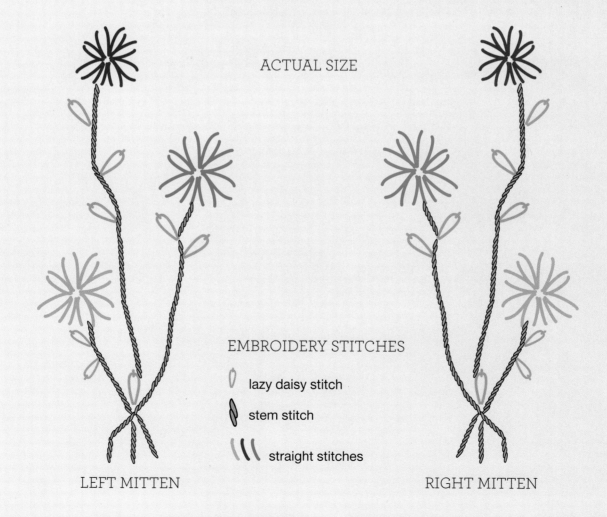

ACTUAL SIZE

EMBROIDERY STITCHES

lazy daisy stitch

stem stitch

straight stitches

LEFT MITTEN

RIGHT MITTEN

Lacy Cables Cap

Lacy Cables Cap

Designed by Lisa Craig

Widely spaced crossover cables are lightened up with laddered lace in this sweet, close-fitting cap.

Skill Level
■■■□

Size
Instructions are written for one size.

Knitted Measurements
Circumference (unstretched) 18"/45.5cm
Height 7½"/19cm

Materials
- 1 3½oz/100g ball (each approx 328yd/300m) of Noro *Silk Garden Sock* (wool/silk/polyamide/mohair) in #399 Greens/Wine (2)
- Two sets (5) (or one set (5) plus one extra needle) each sizes 3 and 6 (3.25 and 4mm) double-pointed needles (dpn), OR SIZE TO OBTAIN GAUGE
- Stitch marker
- Cable needle (cn)

Stitch Glossary
4-st RC Sl 2 sts to cn and hold to *back*, k2, then k2 from cn.
4-st RPC Sl 2 sts to cn and hold to *back*, k2, then p2 from cn.
4-st LPC Sl 2 sts to cn and hold to *front*, p2, then k2 from cn.

Gauge
24 sts and 32 rnds to 4"/10cm over cable and lace pat using larger needles. TAKE TIME TO CHECK GAUGE.

Note
After working the double yo on the chart, on the next rnd, drop the extra yo when working a k1 into this st.

Cap
With smaller dpn, cast on 110 sts, dividing sts evenly over five needles. Join to work in rnds taking care not to twist sts, and pm to mark beg of rnd.
Rnd 1 Work rnd 1 of cable and lace chart, work the 22-st rep 5 times (1 rep on each dpn).
Cont to foll chart in this way through rnd 8.
Change to larger dpn and work through rnd 14. Then, work the 14-rnd rep twice more.
Piece measures approx 5½"/14 cm from beg.

Crown Shaping
Dec rnd 1 [K2, yo, SKP, p1, k2, yo twice, p2tog, k2, (p2tog) twice, k2, p2tog, yo twice, k2, p1] 5 times—100 sts.
Rnd 2 [K2tog, yo, k2, p1, k3, p1, k2, p2, k2, p1, k3, p1] 5 times.
Dec rnd 3 [K2, yo, SKP, p1, k2tog, yo twice, p2tog, k2, p2, k2, p2tog, yo twice, k2tog, p1] 5 times—90 sts.
Rnd 4 [K2tog, yo, k2, (p1, k2) twice, p2, (k2, p1) twice] 5 times.
Dec rnd 5 [K2, yo, SKP, k2tog, yo twice, p2tog, k2, p2, k2, p2tog, yo twice, SKP] 5 times—80 sts.
Rnd 6 [K2tog, yo, k4, p1, k2, p2, k2, p1, k2] 5 times.
Dec rnd 7 [K2, yo, SKP, k1, p2tog, k2, p2, k2, p2tog, k1] 5 times—70 sts.
Rnd 8 [K2tog, yo, k3, p1, k2, p2, k2, p1, k1] 5 times.
Dec rnd 9 [K2, yo, SKP, k1, p1, k1, SKP, k2tog, k1, p1, k1] 5 times—60 sts.
Rnd 10 [K2tog, yo, k3, p1, k4, p1, k1] 5 times.
Dec rnd 11 [K2, yo, SKP, p2tog, 4-st RC, p2tog] 5 times—50 sts.
Rnd 12 [K2tog, yo, k2, p1, k4, p1] 5 times.
Dec rnd 13 [K2, yo, SKP, k2tog, k2, SKP] 5 times—40 sts.

Rnd 14 [K2tog, yo, k6] 5 times.
Dec rnd 15 [K2, yo, SKP, (k2tog) twice] 5 times—30 sts.
Rnd 16 [K2tog, yo, k4] 5 times.
Dec rnd 17 [K2, yo, SKP, k2tog] 5 times—25 sts.
Dec rnd 18 [K2tog, k3] 5 times—20 sts.
Cut yarn, leaving a long end. Pull through sts on needles once, then pull through sts again and draw up tightly to close top.

Finishing
Weave in ends and block hat to knitted measurements. ✤

CABLE AND LACE CHART

22-st rep

STITCH KEY

☐ knit

− purl

O yo

∞ yo twice

◿ k2tog

◺ SKP

◿ p2tog

4-st RC

4-st RPC

4-st LPC

Technology Cover

Technology Cover

Designed by Pat Olski

When it's time-out for your device, put it to sleep in security and style with your custom-knit grill-work design cover.

Skill Level
■■□□

Size
Instructions are written for one size.

Knitted Measurements
Width 8"/20.5cm
Depth 11½"/24cm

Materials
- 1 3½oz/100g ball (each approx 328yd/300m) of Noro *Silk Garden Sock* (wool/silk/polyamide/mohair) in #399 Greens/Wine (A)
- 1 3½oz/100g ball (each approx 328yd/300m) of Noro *Silk Garden Sock Solo* (wool/silk/polyamide/mohair) in #4 Olive Green (B)
- One pair size 1 (2.25mm) needles, OR SIZE TO OBTAIN GAUGE
- Stitch marker
- One ¾"/20mm decorative dome button

Gauge
26 sts and 31 rows to 4"/10cm over St st and color pat chart using size 1 (2.25mm) needles. TAKE TIME TO CHECK GAUGE.

Note
When changing colors foll chart, twist yarns tog at color changes to avoid holes in work, and strand the alternate color loosely across back of work to keep the fabric from puckering

Cover
With A, cast on 104 sts.
Set-up row (RS) With A, k52, pm, k52. Then purl 1 row, knit 1 row with A.

Begin Color Chart
Row 1 (WS) With A, purl.
Row 2 (RS) K1 (selvage st), work row 2 of chart pat over 51 sts, sl marker, work row 2 of chart pat over 51 sts, k1 (selvage st). Then, work rows 3–22 of chart pat once; then work the 20-row rep (or rows 23–42) twice; then work rows 63–79 once. Then, working with A only, work 3 rows even in St st. Cut A.
Next row (WS) With B, *k1, p1; rep from * to end.
Cont in k1, p1 rib with B for 6 rows more.
Next row (RS) Bind off 73 sts tightly, then working on the next 9 sts only for the button tab (and leave the rem sts on hold), work as foll:

Tab
Row 1 (RS) P1 [k1, p1] 4 times, turn. Cont in k1, p1 rib for the tab for 2"/5cm, end with a WS row.
Buttonhole row 1 (RS) P1, k1, p1, k1, yo, k2tog, p1, k1, p1.
Buttonhole row 2 (WS) Rib to the yo, drop the yo and work another yo, rib to end.
Buttonhole row 3 (RS) Rib to the yo space, insert needle under the 2 yo's and p 1 st through these strands, rib to end.
Cont in k1, p1 rib for 3 rows more. Bind off tightly. Rejoin B to the last 22 sts on hold and bind off these sts tightly.

Finishing
Block piece to knitted measurements. Fold in half, sew bottom and side seams to form the case. Sew on button to the front, at the base of the rib, opposite the tab's buttonhole. ❖

COLOR CHART

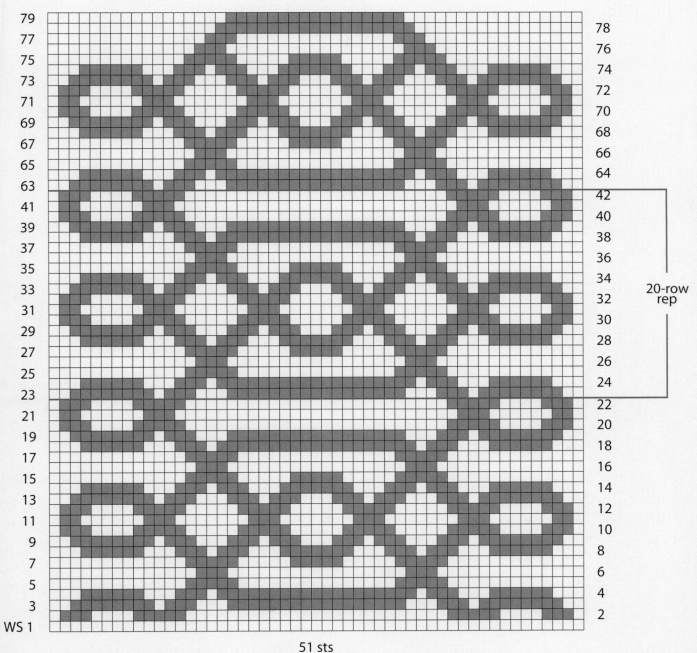

Left side (bottom to top): WS 1, 3, 5, 7, 9, 11, 13, 15, 17, 19, 21, 23, 25, 27, 29, 31, 33, 35, 37, 39, 41, 63, 65, 67, 69, 71, 73, 75, 77, 79

Right side (bottom to top): 2, 4, 6, 8, 10, 12, 14, 16, 18, 20, 22, 24, 26, 28, 30, 32, 34, 36, 38, 40, 42, 64, 66, 68, 70, 72, 74, 76, 78

20-row rep

51 sts

COLOR KEY   ☐ A   ◼ B

Ruffled-Edge Scarf

Ruffled-Edge Scarf

Designed by Lisa Craig

The grid lace pattern at the center of this scarf is anchored by garter trim on all four edges, ending with a flourish of wider ruffles at each end.

Skill Level

■■□□

Size
Instructions are written for one size.

Knitted Measurements
Length 59"/150cm
Width 6¼"/16cm at center; 13"/33cm at ends

Materials
- 4 1¾oz/50 g balls (each approx 137yd/124m) of *Noro Silk Garden Lite* (silk/mohair/wool) in #2082 Green/Gold/Blue/Sienna ⓛ
- One pair size 7 (4.5mm) needles, OR SIZE TO OBTAIN GAUGE
- Size 7 (4.5mm) crochet hook
- Waste yarn

Gauge
18 sts and 28 rows to 4"/10cm over grid lace and garter st pat using size 7 (4.5mm) needles. TAKE TIME TO CHECK GAUGE.

Provisional Cast-on
Using waste yarn and crochet hook, chain the number of sts to cast on, plus a few extra. Cut a tail and pull the tail through the last chain. With knitting needle and working yarn, pick up and knit the stated number of sts through the "purl bumps" on the back of the chain. To remove waste yarn chain, when instructed, pull out the tail from the last crochet stitch. Gently and slowly pull on the tail to unravel the crochet stitches, carefully placing each released knit stitch on the knitting needle.

Scarf
With crochet hook and waste yarn, chain 32. Then, with needles, using the provisional cast-on method, pick up and k 28 sts with the working yarn.

Begin Grid Lace and Garter Stitch
Row 1 (RS) K8, *k2, yo twice, k2; rep from * to last 8 sts, end k8.
Row 2 (WS) K8, *k2tog, (k1, p1) into the double yo, k2tog; rep from * to the last 8 sts, end k8.
Row 3 K8, yo, *k4, yo twice; rep from * to the last 8 sts, end yo, k8.
Row 4 K8, k1 into the yo, [(k2tog) twice, (k1, p1) into the double yo] twice, (k2tog) twice, k1 into the yo, k8.
Rep rows 1–4 until piece measures approx 43"/109cm from beg, end with pat row 2.
**Work 8 rows in garter st (k every row).
Inc row (RS) Kfb 27 times, k1—55 sts.
Purl 1 row, knit 1 row, purl 1 row.

Begin Ruffle Pattern Stitch
Row 1 (RS) [K1, yo, k8, yo] 6 times, k1—67 sts.
Row 2 (WS) [K2, p8, k1] 6 times, k1.
Row 3 [K2, yo, k8, yo, k1] 6 times, k1—79 sts.
Row 4 [K3, p8, k2] 6 times, k1.
Row 5 [K3, yo, k8, yo, k2] 6 times, k1—91 sts.
Row 6 [K4, p8, k3] 6 times, k1.
Row 7 [K4, (k4tog) twice, k3] 6 times, k1—55 sts.
Row 8 Knit.
Rep the last 8 rows 5 times more.
Knit 2 rows.
Bind off loosely. **

Return to the sts at the cast-on edge. Carefully remove the waste yarn and place live sts onto needle.
Rep from ** to ** for the ruffle pat st at the opposite end of the scarf.

Finishing
Weave in ends and block scarf to knitted measurements. ❖

Puff Lace Cowl

Puff Lace Cowl

Designed by Angela Tong

This beautiful cowl, inspired by flower fields that carpet the cliffs and moors of Northern coasts, knits up easily in the round.

Skill Level
■■□□

Size
Instructions are written for one size.

Knitted Measurements
Circumference 39"/99cm
Height 6½"/16.5cm

Materials
■ 2 1¾oz/50g balls (each approx 110yd/100m) of Noro *Silk Garden* (silk/mohair/wool) in #403 Greens/Rust/Navy/Gold 〔4〕
■ One size 9 (5.5mm) circular needle, 32"/80cm long, OR SIZE TO OBTAIN GAUGE
■ Stitch marker

Gauge
12 sts and 22 rnds to 4"/10cm over puff lace pat, after blocking, using size 9 (5.5mm) needle. TAKE TIME TO CHECK GAUGE.

Puff Lace Pattern Stitch
(multiple of 4 sts)
Rnd 1 *P1, k1tbl, p1, yo, k1, yo; rep from * around—2 sts inc'd with each 4-st rep.
Rnd 2 *P1, k1tbl, p1, k3; rep from * around.
Rnd 3 Rep rnd 2.
Rnd 4 *P1, k1tbl, p1, k3tog; rep from * around—2 sts dec'd with each 4-st rep; sts return to original st count.
Rep rnds 1–4 for puff lace pat st.

Cowl
Cast on 120 sts. Join to work in rnds, taking care not to twist sts, and pm to mark beg of rnd.
Knit 1 rnd, purl 1 rnd, knit 1 rnd, purl 1 rnd (for 4 rnds in garter st).
Begin Puff Lace Pattern Stitch
Work in puff lace pat st for 32 rnds (or 8 reps of the 4-rnd pat).
Then, purl 1 rnd, knit 1 rnd, purl 1 rnd, knit 1 rnd (for 4 rnds in garter st).
Bind off loosely knitwise.

Finishing
Weave in ends and block finished piece to knitted measurements. ❖

Orchis Shawl

Orchis Shawl

Designed by Manda Shah

Based on a simple Estonian lace pattern and knit at a loose gauge, this crescent-shaped shawl is as light and airy as butterfly wings.

Skill Level
■ ■ ■ □

Size
Instructions are written for one size.

Knitted Measurements
Wingspan 83"/210cm
Height 24"/61cm

Materials
- 2 3½oz/100g balls (each approx 328yd/300m) of Noro *Silk Garden Sock Solo* (wool/silk/polyamide/mohair) in #10 Pink (2)
- One size 7 (4.5mm) circular needle, 32"/80cm long, OR SIZE TO OBTAIN GAUGE

Gauges
16 sts and 19 rows to 4"/10cm over St st, after wet blocking, using size 7 (4.5mm) needle;
12 sts and 20 rows to 4"/10cm over lace pat foll chart, after wet blocking, using size 7 (4.5mm) needle. TAKE TIME TO CHECK GAUGES.

Note
Charts can be found on page 140.

Shawl
Begin the shawl at the lower edge with a garter tab cast-on, as foll:
Cast on 2 sts using the knitted cast-on method. Knit 3 rows.
Turn to work along side of tab as foll:
Row 1 (RS) Working into the end of the row, yo, pick up and k 1 st from the garter ridge, yo, pick up and k the 2 cast-on sts—7 sts.
Row 2 (WS) K2, p3, k2.
Row 3 K2, [yo, k1] 3 times, yo, k2—11 sts.
Row 4 K2, p7, k2.

Begin Chart 1
Beg with row 1, work through row 12 of chart 1—39 sts.

Begin Chart 2
Row 1 (RS) Beg with the first st of row 1, work to the rep, work the 14-st rep across, ending with the sts after the rep. (**Note** Each 6-row rep of chart 2 adds 14 sts to the st count.) Cont to foll chart 2 in this way until a total of 17 reps of the 6-row rep have been completed—277 sts.

Begin Chart 3
Row 1 (RS) Beg with the first st of row 1, work to the rep, work the 14-st rep across, ending with the sts after the rep. Cont to foll chart 3 through row 8. Bind off all sts *loosely*.

Finishing
Weave in ends and block shawl to measurements, pinning scalloped edge into shape. Trim ends after blocking. ❧

DIAGRAM

3½"

3½"

open from here ⟶

17"

14"

open from here

14"

LEGEND/ DIRECTION

△ base triangles with A ←   ▶ 2nd row end triangle with A ←
◆ first row squares with B →   ◆ 3rd row squares with B →
◀ 2nd row beg triangle with A ←   ▽ top RS triangle with A ←
◆ 2nd row squares with A ←   ▽ top WS triangle with B →

Japanese Knot Bag (*page 26*)

Finishing
Weave in ends and block pieces to measurements.
Sew the strap seams tog at top. Sew the front and back of the bag on all 3 sides, up to the handle openings. Weave in ends.

Lining
Using the bag's shape as a template, cut 2 pieces of fabric with a ¾"/2cm seam allowance on all sides. Using a sewing machine, with right sides together, sew the pieces together along the 3 sides of the lining that make up the U-shape that ends at strap openings.

Sew the strap seams tog at top. Turn a ¾"/2cm seam allowance and baste. The rem of the lining will be hand sewn to the bag when it is completed. Make a machine-stitched enclosure for one cut 6"/15cm piece of the flexible plastic strip at the lining center at 1"/2.5cm from the top and centered on each top center lining piece. Insert the plastic strip inside this enclosure and stitch at both ends to hold in place. Fold and press the lining along the seam allowance line, and hand sew to the handles and along both top edges of the bag. Leave the inside lining at the bottom of the bag free. ❖

Drape Front Cardigan (*page 30*)

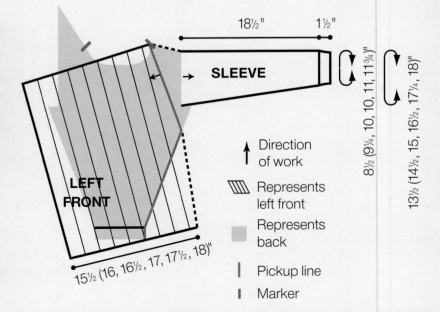

18½"   1½"

SLEEVE

8½ (9¼, 10, 10, 11, 11¾)"

13½ (14½, 15, 16½, 17¼, 18)"

LEFT FRONT

↑ Direction of work

▨ Represents left front

▨ Represents back

| Pickup line

▮ Marker

15½ (16, 16½, 17, 17½, 18)"

Modular Pieced Cape *(page 50)*

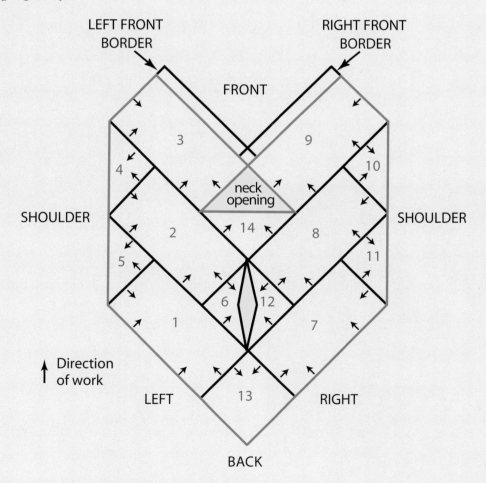

LEFT FRONT
BORDER

RIGHT FRONT
BORDER

FRONT

3

9

4

10

neck
opening

SHOULDER

SHOULDER

2

14

8

5

11

6   12

1

7

↑ Direction
   of work

LEFT

13

RIGHT

BACK

CHART 1

39 sts

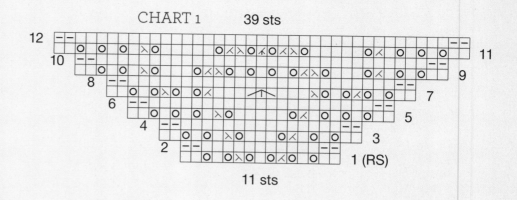

11 sts

CHART 2

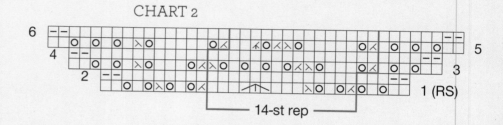

14-st rep

CHART 3

12 sts

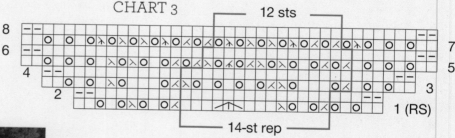

14-st rep

Orchis Shawl (*page 134*)

STITCH KEY

☐ k on RS, p on WS

▭ p on RS, k on WS

⊙ yo

⊠ k2tog

⊠ SKP

⊠ k3tog

⊠ SK2P

⟋⟋⟍ k3 sts tog, do not sl from needle, yo, k3tog again and sl the sts from LH needle

Helpful Information

Abbreviations

approx	approximately
beg	begin(ning)
CC	contrasting color
ch	chain
cm	centimeter(s)
cn	cable needle
cont	continu(e)(ing)
dec	decreas(e)(ing)
dpn(s)	double-pointed needle(s)
foll	follow(s)(ing)
g	gram(s)
inc	increase(e)(ing)
k	knit
k2tog	knit 2 stitches together
kfb	knit into front and back of stitch
LH	left-hand
lp(s)	loop(s)
m	meter(s)
MB	make bobble
MC	main color
mm	millimeter(s)
M1 or M1L	make one or make one left (see glossary)
M1 p-st	make 1 purl stitch (see glossary)
M1R	make one right (see glossary)
oz	ounce(s)
p	purl
p2tog	purl 2 stitches together
pat(s)	pattern(s)

pm	place marker
psso	pass slip stitch(es) over
rem	remain(s)(ing)
rep	repeat(s)(ing)(ed)
RH	right-hand
rnd(s)	round(s)
RS	right side(s)
S2KP	slip 2 stitches together knitwise, knit 1, pass 2 slip stitches over knit 1 for a centered double decrease
SK2P	slip 1 knitwise, knit 2 together, pass slip stitch over the knit 2 together for a left-slanting double decrease
SKP	slip 1 knitwise, knit 1, pass slip stitch over
sl	slip
sl st	slip stitch
ssk	slip, slip, knit (see glossary)
ssp	slip the next 2 sts one at a time purlwise to RH needle, insert tip of LH needle into fronts of these sts and purl them together
sssk	see glossary
st(s)	stitch(es)
St st	stockinette stitch
tbl	through back loop(s)
tog	together
w&t	wrap and turn
WS	wrong side(s)
wyib	with yarn in back
wyif	with yarn in front
yd	yard(s)
yo	yarn over needle
*	repeat directions following * as many times as indicated
[]	repeat directions inside brackets as many times as indicated

Checking Your Gauge

Make a test swatch at least 4"/10cm square. If the number of stitches and rows does not correspond to the gauge given, you must change the needle size. An easy rule to follow is: To get fewer stitches to the inch/cm, use a larger needle; to get more stitches to the inch/cm, use a smaller needle. Continue to try different needle sizes until you get the same number of stitches in the gauge.

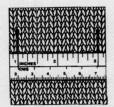

Stitches measured over 2"/5cm

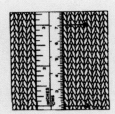

Rows measured over 2"/5cm

Skill Levels

■□□□
Beginner
Ideal first project.

■■□□
Easy
Basic stitches, minimal shaping, and simple finishing.

■■■□
Intermediate
For knitters with some experience. More intricate stitches, shaping, and finishing.

■■■■
Experienced
For knitters able to work patterns with complicated shaping and finishing.

Knitting Needle Sizes

U.S.	Metric	U.S.	Metric
0	2mm	10	6mm
1	2.25mm	10½	6.5mm
2	2.75mm	11	8mm
3	3.25mm	13	9mm
4	3.5mm	15	10mm
5	3.75mm	17	12.75mm
6	4mm	19	15mm
7	4.5mm	35	19mm
8	5mm		
9	5.5mm		

Standard Yarn Weight System

Categories of yarn, gauge ranges, and recommended needle and hook sizes

Yarn Weight Symbol & Category Names	(0) Lace	(1) Super Fine	(2) Fine	(3) Light	(4) Medium	(5) Bulky	(6) Super Bulky
Type of Yarns in Category	Fingering 10 count crochet thread	Sock, Fingering, Baby	Sport, Baby	DK, Light Worsted	Worsted, Afghan, Aran	Chunky, Craft, Rug	Bulky, Roving
Knit Gauge Range* in Stockinette Stitch to 4 inches	33–40** sts	27–32 sts	23–26 sts	21–24 sts	16–20 sts	12–15 sts	6–11 sts
Recommended Needle in Metric Size Range	1.5–2.25 mm	2.25–3.25 mm	3.25–3.75 mm	3.75–4.5 mm	4.5–5.5 mm	5.5–8 mm	8 mm and larger
Recommended Needle U.S. Size Range	000 to 1	1 to 3	3 to 5	5 to 7	7 to 9	9 to 11	11 and larger
Crochet Gauge* Ranges in Single Crochet to 4 inch	32-42 double crochets**	21–32 sts	16–20 sts	12–17 sts	11–14 sts	8–11 sts	5–9 sts
Recommended Hook in Metric Size Range	Steel*** 1.6–1.4mm Regular hook 2.25 mm	2.25–3.5 mm	3.5–4.5 mm	4.5–5.5 mm	5.5–6.5 mm	6.5–9 mm	9 mm and larger
Recommended Hook U.S. Size Range	Steel*** 6, 7, 8 Regular hook B–1	B–1 to E–4	E–4 to 7	7 to I–9	I–9 to K–10½	K–10½ to M–13	M–13 and larger

*GUIDELINES ONLY: The above reflect the most commonly used gauges and needle or hook sizes for specific yarn categories.

**Lace weight yarns are usually knitted or crocheted on larger needles and hooks to create lacy, openwork patterns. Accordingly, a gauge range is difficult to determine. Always follow the gauge stated in your pattern.

*** Steel crochet hooks are sized differently from regular hooks: the higher the number, the smaller the hook, which is the reverse of regular hook sizing. This Standards & Guidelines booklet and downloadable symbol artwork are available at YarnStandards.com.

Glossary

as foll Work the instructions that follow.

bind off Used to finish an edge or segment. Lift the first stitch over the second, the second over the third, etc. (U.K.: cast off)

bind off in ribbing Work in ribbing as you bind off. (Knit the knit stitches, purl the purl stitches.) (U.K.: cast off in ribbing)

3-needle bind-off With the right side of the two pieces facing and the needles parallel, insert a third needle into the first stitch on each needle and knit them together. Knit the next two stitches the same way. Slip the first stitch on the third needle over the second stitch and off the needle. Repeat for three-needle bind-off.

cast on Placing a foundation row of stitches upon the needle in order to begin knitting.

decrease Reduce the stitches in a row (that is, knit 2 together).

hold to front (back) of work Usually refers to stitches placed on a cable needle that are held to the front (or back) of the work as it faces you.

increase Add stitches in a row (that is, knit in front and back of stitch).

knitwise Insert the needle into the stitch as if you were going to knit it.

make one or make one left Insert left-hand needle from front to back under the strand between last stitch worked and next stitch on left-hand needle. Knit into back loop. One knit stitch has been added.

make one p-st With the needle tip, lift the strand between the last stitch worked and the next stitch on the left-hand needle and purl it. One purl stitch has been added.

make one right Insert left-hand needle from back to front under the strand between last stitch worked and next stitch on left-hand needle. Knit into front loop. One knit stitch has been added.

no stitch On some charts, "no stitch" is indicated with shaded spaces where stitches have been decreased or not yet made. In such cases, work the stitches of the chart, skipping over the "no stitch" spaces.

place markers Place or attach a loop of contrast yarn or purchased stitch marker as indicated.

pick up and knit (purl) Knit (or purl) into the loops along an edge.

purlwise Insert the needle into the stitch as if you were going to purl it.

selvage stitch Edge stitch that helps make seaming easier.

slip, slip, knit Slip next two stitches knitwise, one at a time, to right-hand needle. Insert tip of left-hand needle into fronts of these stitches, from left to right. Knit them together. One stitch has been decreased.

slip, slip, slip, knit Slip next three stitches knitwise, one at a time, to right-hand needle. Insert tip of left-hand needle into fronts of these stitches, from left to right. Knit them together. Two stitches have been decreased.

slip stitch An unworked stitch made by passing a stitch from the left-hand to the right-hand needle as if to purl.

stockinette stitch Knit every right-side row and purl every wrong-side row.

work even Continue in pattern without increasing or decreasing. (U.K.: work straight)

work to end Work the established pattern to the end of the row.

yarn over Making a new stitch by wrapping the yarn over the right-hand needle. (U.K.: yfwd, yon, yrn)

Distributors

To locate retailers of Noro yarns, please contact one of the following distributors:

USA

Knitting Fever Inc.

315 Bayview Avenue

Amityville, New York 11701

Tel: 001 516 546 3600

Fax: 001 516 546 6871

www.knittingfever.com

UK & EUROPE

Designer Yarns Ltd.

Units 8-10

Newbridge Industrial Estate

Pitt Street

Keighley BD21 4PQ

UNITED KINGDOM

Tel: +44 (0)1535 664222

Fax: +44 (0)1535 664333

Email: alex@designeryarns.uk.com

www.designeryarns.uk.com

GERMANY / AUSTRIA / SWITZERLAND / BELGIUM / NETHERLANDS / LUXEMBOURG

Designer Yarns (Deutschland) GMBH

Welserstrasse 10g

D-51149 Koln

GERMANY

Tel: +49 (0) 2203 1021910

Fax: +49 (0) 2203 1023551

Email: info@designeryarns.de

Index